Suno AI for Everyone

A Step-by-Step Guide to Mastering This AI Music

By

Marcelo Honores

Contents

Introduction	6
Have You Ever Dreamed of Making Music?	6
Introducing Your New Musical Partner: Suno AI	7
A Guide Designed for the Absolute Beginner	7
Our Roadmap: From Zero to Composer	8
Let's Start to Make Music Now	9
Chapter 1: Getting Started with the Suno Platform	10
Welcome to the Suno Platform	10
Creating Your Suno Account	11
Suno's Subscription Plans	11
Exploring the Suno Interface	12
Suggestions to Organizing Your Music	13
Case Study	14
Homework	15
Chapter Summary	15
Chapter 2: Understanding Simple Mode	16
Defining Simple Mode?	16
Elements of Simple Mode Screen	17
Writing Song Descriptions	17
A Handy Template for Simple Mode Prompts	18
Adding Titles to Your Songs	18
Create Simple Mode Instrumental Songs	19
Case Study	19
Homework	21
Chapter Summary	22
Chapter 3: Understanding Suno's Custom Mode	23
Defining Custom Mode	23
Starting with Custom Mode	24
Main Components of Custom Mode	24
Introduction to Lyrics Creation	25

The 3 Ways to Create Lyrics	26
Creating Music with Style Prompts	26
Style Prompt Template	27
Advanced Topics	27
Case Study	28
Homework	29
Chapter Summary	30
Chapter 4: Learn to Compose Music with Style Prompts	31
Defining Style Prompts	31
Building Blocks of a Style Prompt	32
Emphasis Techniques	35
Style Prompt Templates	37
Case Study	39
Homework	40
Chapter Summary	41
Chapter 5: Learn to Create Lyrics with Metatags	42
Defining Metatags	42
Structural Metatags	43
Basic Song Sections	43
Transitional & Instrumental Sections	45
Ending Tags	46
Instrumental Performance	46
Vocal Delivery	47
Styling Vocals	47
Templates to Create Lyrics	48
Case Study	50
Homework	53
Chapter Summary	54
Chapter 6: Personalize Songs with Lyric Formatters	55
Definition of Lyric Formatters	55
Punctuation for Pauses and Phrasing	56
Line Breaks for Rhythmic Pauses	57

Capitalization for Emphasis ... 57
Asterisks for Whispers and Echoes ... 58
Parentheses for Ad-Libs and Asides ... 59
Vocal Metatags for Flow ... 59
Case Study: All Lyric Formatters in Action ... 61
Homework ... 62
Chapter Summary ... 63

Chapter 7: How to Create Catchy Songs ... 64

Unlocking the Psychology of Catchiness ... 64
    "Normal" Songs vs. "Catchy" Songs ... 66
The Repetitive Metatags Review ... 66
The Seven Key Ingredients of Catchiness ... 67
Balancing the Catchy Elements ... 68
Tips to Making it Catchy in Suno ... 69
Catchy Prompt Templates ... 70
    A. Template to Generate Catchy Lyrics: ... 70
    B. Template to Generate Catchy Music: ... 71
Case Study: Taking "I Won the Lottery" from Basic to Super-Catchy ... 72
Homework & Practice ... 76
Chapter Summary ... 77

Chapter 8: Reverse Engineering Popular Songs ... 78

Defining Reverse Engineering ... 78
Ethical Considerations: Inspiration vs. Imitation ... 79
Choosing a Famous Song ... 79
Active Listening ... 80
Extracting Key Lyrics Elements from a Song ... 81
    Template prompt for lyrics analysis: ... 81
Extracting Key Music Elements from a Song ... 83
Personalizing the New Song ... 85
    Lyrics Personalization ... 85
    Music Personalization ... 85
Case Study ... 86

Homework	90
Chapter Summary	90
Chapter 9: From Beats to Bucks - Make Money with Suno	92
Suno can be More Than Just a Hobby	92
What Makes Music Valuable?	93
Ways to Create Value with Custom Music	93
Music is the New Valuable Currency	94
Transitioning from Value to Income	94
Commercial License Requirement	94
Monetization Strategies	95
Building Your Suno Brand	97
Important Considerations for the Suno Entrepreneur	97
Case Study: From Birthday Gift to First Gig	98
Homework	100
Chapter Summary	101
Chatbots of the Book	104
Appendix A: Genres & Subgenres	105
Annex B: Main Suno's Metatags	106
Song Structure Tags	106
Instrumental Tags	107
Vocal Tags	107
Tempo & Dynamics Tags	108
Special Effects Tags	108
Appendix C: Moods for Style Prompts	109
Annex D: Tempo Keywords	110
Annex E: Vocal Keywords	111
Gender & Age	111
Vocal Quality & Texture	111
Singing Style & Delivery	112
Emotional Tone	112
Personas & Characters	112

    Vocal Effects ... 113
Appendix F: Instrument Keywords ... 113

    String Instruments (Guitars & Bass) ... 113
    String Instruments (Orchestral & Folk) ... 114
    Keyboard Instruments ... 114
    Percussion Instruments ... 115
    Wind Instruments ... 115
    Electronic Instruments & Effects ... 115

Appendix G: Sonic Textures ... 116

    Sound Quality & Fidelity ... 116
    Density & Space ... 116
    Atmospheric & Environmental ... 117
    Rhythmic Feel & Movement ... 118

Appendix H: Production Techniques ... 119

    Spatial & Time-Based Effects ... 119
    Modulation & Texture Effects ... 119
    Dynamic & Tonal Shaping ... 120
    Arrangement & Mixing Techniques ... 120

Appendix I: Arrangement & Performance ... 121

    Rhythmic Foundation & Groove ... 121
    Melodic & Harmonic Elements ... 121
    Performance Dynamics & Energy Flow ... 122
    Overall Performance Style ... 123

Introduction

Chapter Outline

- Have You Ever Dreamed of Making Music?
- Introducing Your New Musical Partner: Suno AI
- A Guide Designed for the Absolute Beginner
- Our Roadmap: From Zero to Composer
- Let's Start to Make Music

Have You Ever Dreamed of Making Music?

Have you ever hummed a melody that didn't exist, a perfect little tune that was yours and yours alone? Have you ever wished you could turn a feeling—a moment of joy, a pang of heartbreak, a funny inside joke—into a real song? For most of us, that's where the dream ends.

The path to making music has always been lined with barriers. It meant years of expensive lessons, mastering a difficult instrument, and trying to understand complex music theory. It felt like a special club, and if you weren't born "musical," you weren't getting in. That feeling of having a song trapped inside you with no way to get it out is a frustrating one.

Until now.

Introducing Your New Musical Partner: Suno AI

Imagine a creative partner who is a master of every instrument, knows every genre of music, and is ready to compose 24/7, all based on your ideas. That partner is Suno AI.

Suno is a revolutionary tool that turns your words into music. It's not just a cold machine; it's a collaborator that listens to your descriptions— "a sad acoustic song about a rainy day," "an energetic dance track for a party"—and instantly brings them to life as full-length, professional-sounding songs. All those traditional barriers? Suno removes them. You don't need an instrument. You don't need lessons. All you need is an idea.

A Guide Designed for the Absolute Beginner

You're holding the key to unlocking this incredible technology. This book isn't just a manual; it's your personal tutor, designed specifically for the absolute beginner to make the learning process fun, practical, and incredibly rewarding.

Here's why this book is your perfect guide:

- **Music Theory, Made Simple:** We won't bury you in intimidating sheet music. We'll introduce you to only the essential concepts you need to communicate your ideas effectively, explained in plain English.

- **Learn by Doing, Not Just Reading:** This isn't a lecture; it's a hands-on workshop. Every chapter is filled with practical examples and step-by-step case studies that you can replicate in Suno to see the results for yourself.

- **Creative Shortcuts with Templates:** Staring at a blank page is scary. That's why we've included ready-to-use templates you can use with chatbots to generate lyrics and musical styles, giving you a perfect starting point for your own creations.

- **Your 24/7 AI Teaching Assistant:** Got a question at 2 AM? We've got you covered. This book comes with its own free companion chatbot, designed to answer your questions anytime so you never get stuck.

- **Your Personal "Cheat Sheets":** Don't worry about memorizing hundreds of keywords. The appendixes at the end of this book act as your quick-reference library for genres, moods, instruments, and more.

- **A Path to Profit:** We believe your creativity has value. That's why we've included a whole chapter on how you can potentially turn this fun new hobby into a source of income.

- **Skills for the Future:** The principles you learn here aren't just for Suno. AI music is a rapidly growing field, and this book will give you a foundational understanding that applies to other amazing tools like Udio and whatever comes next.

Our Roadmap: From Zero to Composer

This book will take you on a structured journey. We've broken down the learning process into three simple parts, each building on the last.

- **Part 1: The Foundation (Chapters 1-3):** You'll start with the absolute basics. We'll get you set up on the platform and introduce you to Suno's core creation modes, ensuring you have a solid and confident start.

- **Part 2: The Creative Toolkit (Chapters 4-6):** This is where you become the artist. You'll learn to master Style Prompts, Metatags, and Lyric Formatters—the tools that let you shape every detail of your sound, from the genre to the vocal delivery.

- **Part 3: The Path to Mastery (Chapters 7-9):** You'll put your skills to the test. You will learn the secrets of creating catchy songs, how to reverse-engineer your favorite hits, and how to monetize your music.

Let's Start to Make Music Now

The only thing missing from this incredible new world of music is you. Your ideas, your stories, your voice. The future of music is here, it's accessible to everyone, and it's waiting for you to press "Create."

Let's get started.

Chapter 1: Getting Started with the Suno Platform

Welcome to the exciting world of AI-powered music creation! This chapter is your guide to getting started with Suno, an innovative tool that lets you generate original music even if you've never played a note in your life. We'll cover everything from creating your account to exploring Suno's interface and generating your first AI-powered melodies. By the end of this chapter, you'll be comfortable with the basics and ready to begin your musical adventure.

Chapter Outline

- Welcome to the Suno Platform
- Creating Your Suno Account
- Suno's Subscription Plans
- Exploring the Suno Interface
- Suggestions to Organizing Your Music
- Smart Naming Tips
- Case Study
- Homework

Welcome to the Suno Platform

Imagine composing a powerful symphony, producing a chart-topping hit song, or creating a soundtrack for your very own film—all without years of musical training. This isn't a fantasy; it's the reality of AI-powered music creation. At the forefront of this revolution is Suno, a remarkably intuitive AI music generator that turns your ideas into captivating songs. It's like having a talented musical partner who's always ready to collaborate.

Creating Your Suno Account

The first step is simple: head over to **Suno.com** and create a free account. Click the "Sign Up" button, and you can choose to log in quickly using your Google or Apple account. If you prefer, you can enter your email address and set up a password.

Suno's Subscription Plans

Suno AI offers a few subscription plans designed for different types of users, from curious beginners to serious creators.

The **Basic Plan** is completely free and the perfect way to get your feet wet. It gives you 50 credits each day, which is enough to make about 10 songs. This is great for learning the platform, but keep in mind that any music you make is for non-commercial use only. You'll also be in a shared line for song generation, so it might be a bit slower during busy times.

The **Pro Plan** costs about $10 per month and is ideal for hobbyists who want more creative freedom. You get a big batch of 2,500 credits each month (that's about 500 songs!) and, most importantly, the right to use your songs commercially. This plan also puts you in a priority queue for faster generation and gives you access to Suno's latest AI models and tools. A good tip is to sign up for the free plan first and keep an eye out for special discount offers they might send you.

The **Premier Plan** is for professional musicians and high-volume creators. For about $30 a month, you get all the benefits of the Pro plan but with a massive 10,000 credits, enough to generate around 2,000 songs monthly.

You can also earn up to 2,500 free credits by inviting friends to join Suno. If you're on a paid plan and run out of credits, you can buy more. Just remember, your monthly credits don't roll over, so be sure to use them!

Exploring the Suno Interface

Once you're logged in, you'll see Suno's user-friendly interface. Let's take a quick tour of the main menu on the left side:

- **User Profile:** This is where you can see statistics about your music, like how many people have played your songs.

- **Home:** This is your landing page. Here, you'll find trending songs and curated playlists. It's a great source of inspiration.

- **Create:** This is where the magic happens! The "Create" section is your music studio, providing all the tools you need to generate songs.

- **Library:** Think of this as your musical library. All the songs and playlists you create will be stored here.

- **Explore:** Want to discover new music? The "Explore" section lets you browse Suno's huge catalog of AI-generated songs.

- **Search:** Looking for something specific? Use the search bar to find music based on keywords or genres.

- **Notifications:** This is where you'll find updates and alerts about your account.

- **Credits:** This displays how many credits you have left to generate songs.

- **Invite friends:** Use this to send invitations to your friends and earn extra credits.

- **What's new:** Suno is always adding new features. Stay up-to-date with the latest developments in this section.

- **More from Suno:** Here you can find useful resources, including the **Help** section, which provides clear explanations and answers to frequently asked questions.

Suggestions to Organizing Your Music

As you start creating, you'll want to keep your projects organized. Suno gives you two main ways to do this:

- **Workspaces:** Think of these like folders on your computer. They are for your eyes only and are great for keeping different projects or ideas separate.

- **Playlists:** These work just like playlists on any streaming service. You can make them private or public, which is perfect for sharing your music with others.

Here are a few ideas for organizing your work:

- **By Project:** If you're working on an album or a series of singles, create a dedicated workspace or playlist for it.

- **By Genre:** Group your songs by style, like Pop, Rock, or EDM. This makes it easy to find a specific vibe when you need it.

- **Songs You Like:** Create a playlist of songs you find inspiring to keep your creative juices flowing.

- **By Learning:** A fantastic way to improve is to learn from others. Create a playlist called "Illustrative Songs" and save any songs that have interesting techniques you'd like to study later.

Smart Naming Tips

Using consistent and descriptive names for your songs and playlists will make them much easier to find and manage. It's a good habit to document your work.

- **For Songs:** Use a title that clearly reflects the song's theme or content. A good template is: [Song Name] - [Genre] - [Purpose]. For example: "Summer Memories - Pop - Album Demo" or "City at Night - Jazz - Instrumental".

- **For Playlists:** Use names that clearly indicate the playlist's purpose. A simple template is: [Name] - [Purpose]. For example: "Upbeat Rock Anthems" or "My Lofi Collection - For Study".

Case Study

Let's put this into practice. Go to the **Library** section in Suno and create a new playlist. Name it "Illustrative Songs". Now, go to the **Explore** or **Home** page and search for three songs that catch your ear. Listen to them, and if you think they do something cool, add them to your new "Illustrative Songs" playlist. This will be your personal library of great examples to learn from as you progress through this book.

Homework

- **Task 1:** Go to the menu item "More from Suno" and click on the "Help" section. Read through the topics to get a better understanding of the platform's features.

- **Task 2:** Listen to this chapter's companion songs in the book's official playlist here: https://suno.com/playlist/0715eba6-45e6-4fe7-9893-4b38aa7780cc

Questions?

If you have questions about this chapter, ask the book's free companion chatbot. You can find the links in the Resources section of the book.

Chapter Summary

Congratulations! You've taken your first steps into the world of AI-powered music. In this chapter, you learned how to set up your account, what the different subscription plans offer, and how to find your way around the Suno platform. You also learned how to organize your music with workspaces and playlists and the importance of smart naming conventions.

Now that you have a basic understanding of Suno, you're ready to start making more creative and expressive music. In the next chapter, we'll look at "Simple Mode," the easiest way to bring your musical ideas to life.

Chapter 2: Understanding Simple Mode

In the last chapter, you got your bearings on the Suno platform, from setting up your account to organizing your future creations. Now, you're ready to make your first song! In this chapter, we'll explore "Simple Mode," the easiest and fastest way to bring your musical ideas to life. Whether you imagine a catchy song with lyrics or a captivating instrumental piece, Simple Mode is your gateway to creating original music, even without any musical background.

Chapter Outline:

- What is Simple Mode?
- Elements of Simple Mode Screen
- Writing Personalized Song Descriptions
- Case Study: Exploring Simple Mode
- Homework

Defining Simple Mode?

When you click "Create" in Suno's menu, you land directly in Simple Mode. Think of it as the "easy button" for making music. It's designed to be fast and fun, letting you turn a simple idea into a song in moments.

Simple Mode works with a single text prompt. You just type a description of the music you want, and Suno's AI does the heavy lifting. It will interpret your words to choose the genre, instruments, vocals, and even write the lyrics for you.

Keep in mind that the song description box in Simple Mode has a character limit, usually around 200 characters. This encourages you to be clear and concise with your ideas.

Elements of Simple Mode Screen

The Simple Mode screen is clean and focused. Here are the main parts you'll be using:

- **Song Description Box:** This is the main text box where all the magic starts. You type your song idea here.

- **Style Suggestion Button:** Feeling uninspired? Look for the small button on the top-right of the Song Description Box (it often looks like a paste icon or dice). Clicking this will generate random style ideas for you to try out.

- **Style/Genre Suggestion Tags:** Below the main text box, you'll often see several pill-shaped tags with different genres or styles. You can click on these to quickly add them to your song description.

- **Create Button:** Once you've typed your idea, this is the big, colorful button you press to tell Suno to start composing your song.

Writing Song Descriptions

The song description is your instruction manual for Suno's AI. The clearer your prompt, the closer Suno will get to the music you imagine. To create your own personalized song, think about these three elements:

- **Expressing Mood:** Words are powerful! Choose words that capture the feeling you want. Do you want something "joyful" and "upbeat"? Or perhaps "melancholy" and "reflective"? Experiment with words like "intense," "dreamy," "soothing," "powerful," or "playful."

- **Building Scenarios:** Create a musical atmosphere with prompts that tell a story or set a scene. For example, "a lone traveler crossing a desert" paints a clear picture. Try other scenarios, like "a bustling city street at night" or "a celebration under the stars."
- **Using Figurative Language:** Metaphors and similes add depth to your prompts. Instead of "a happy song," you could write "a song that feels like a warm summer breeze." Instead of "a sad melody," try "a melody as fragile as a snowflake."

A Handy Template for Simple Mode Prompts

Here's a simple formula to help you get started: **[Mood] [Genre] song about [Scenario/Story/Theme]**

Examples:

- "A melancholy folk song about a lost love."
- "An energetic EDM track about a futuristic cityscape."
- "A powerful rock anthem about overcoming a personal challenge."
- "A laid-back hip-hop song about a lazy Sunday afternoon."
- "A soulful R&B ballad about reuniting with an old friend."

Adding Titles to Your Songs

In Simple Mode, Suno will automatically assign a title to your song based on your prompt. However, if you want to give your song a specific title, you can! Just add one of the following phrases to the end of your prompt:

- Use the word "titled"
- Use the phrase "with title"

Examples:

- "A joyful children's song about a birthday party, titled 'Happy Birthday.'"
- "A mysterious ambient piece that feels like a deep ocean, titled 'Ocean's Secret'."
- "A romantic piano ballad about a long-lasting relationship, with title 'Anniversary Waltz.'"
- "A fast-paced country song about a road trip, with title 'Highway Miles.'"

Create Simple Mode Instrumental Songs

By default, Suno is ready to create a song with lyrics and vocals. But what if you just want the music? It's simple to switch to instrumental mode.

Below the style box, you'll see an "Instrumental" button. Just click it to activate instrumental mode. The same prompt template works perfectly here, too. Suno will just focus on the music and skip the singing.

Case Study

Let's see Simple Mode in action! We'll start with songs that have lyrics and then check out some instrumental tracks.

Examples for Songs with Lyrics:

- **Prompt:** "A happy pop song about a summer day at the beach."

- ○ **Analysis:** Did Suno capture the cheerful mood with a bright melody and upbeat tempo? Can you hear typical pop instruments like guitars and drums?
- **Prompt:** "A haunting ballad about a ghost searching for lost love."
  - ○ **Analysis:** Did Suno create a slower tempo and a melancholy feel? Did you hear instruments like piano and strings? Are there any spooky sound effects?
- **Prompt:** "A groovy jazz song about a rainy night in New Orleans."
  - ○ **Analysis:** Did Suno use instruments like saxophone, trumpet, and piano to create a jazz vibe? Does the song have a bluesy feel and a syncopated rhythm?

Examples for Instrumental Tracks:

- **Prompt:** "Relaxing ambient music for yoga."
  - ○ **Analysis:** Do you hear calming sounds with slow, drawn-out melodies? Did Suno use instruments like piano, strings, or nature sounds to enhance the mood?
- **Prompt:** "An intense orchestral piece about a storm at sea."
  - ○ **Analysis:** Did Suno create a dramatic piece with a fast tempo and a powerful orchestral sound? Can you hear a variety of instruments, including strings, brass, and percussion?
- **Prompt:** "A whimsical folk melody that feels like dancing through a meadow."

- **Analysis:** Did Suno compose a lighthearted and playful melody? What instruments did it choose to create that feeling of dancing in a meadow?

Homework

- **Task 1:** Run some of the example prompts from the case study in Suno. Listen to the results and analyze how well the AI captured the mood, scenario, and feel of each prompt.

- **Task 2:** Now it's your turn! Create three original songs in Simple Mode. Make them about things you personally enjoy. Try to make something nobody else has created yet!

- **Task 3:** Go to your Library and create a new playlist called "My Examples." Add the songs you just created to this playlist to keep them organized.

- **Task 4:** Spend some time in the 'Explore' section and find five songs made by other users that you think are cool or interesting. Add them to your "Illustrative Songs" playlist.

- **Task 5:** Listen to the song created for this chapter, which you can find in the book's official playlist here: https://suno.com/playlist/0715eba6-45e6-4fe7-9893-4b38aa7780cc

Questions?

If you have questions about anything covered in this chapter, remember you can ask the book's free companion chatbot! You can find the links to the chatbot in the Resources section at the end of the book.

Chapter Summary

In this chapter, you learned all about Suno's Simple Mode. We saw that it's the fastest and easiest way to start making music, using just a single text prompt to get things going. We looked at how to write effective song descriptions by thinking about mood, scenarios, and figurative language. You also learned how to add your own titles and how to switch to instrumental mode.

Simple Mode is a fantastic way to quickly turn your ideas into music. In the next chapter, we'll look at "Custom Mode," where you get even more control over your lyrics and musical style. Get ready to take your Suno skills to a new level

Chapter 3: Understanding Suno's Custom Mode

In the last chapter, you saw how easy it is to make music with Simple Mode. Now, get ready for more control! We're stepping into "Custom Mode," which gives you even more personalization over your music. The big difference? You'll write separate prompts for your **lyrics** and the **musical style**. This means you can fine-tune each element to create songs that perfectly match your creative vision.

Chapter Outline:
- Defining Custom Mode
- Starting with Custom Mode
- Main Components of Custom Mode
- Introduction to Lyrics Creation
- The 3 Ways to Create Lyrics
- Creating Music with Style Prompts
- Template Style Prompt
- Advanced Topics
- Case Study
- Homework

Defining Custom Mode

Custom Mode is the next level of your music-making journey. Unlike Simple Mode, which uses one single description for everything, Custom Mode splits the process into two main parts: one for the words (lyrics) and one for the music (style).

The biggest advantage is control. By separating these elements, you can write your own very specific lyrics and then try them out with completely different musical styles. Want to hear your heartfelt poem as both a heavy metal anthem and a gentle acoustic tune? Custom Mode makes that possible.

Starting with Custom Mode

Finding Custom Mode is a breeze. On the "Create" page, you'll see two tabs at the top: "Simple" and "Custom." Just click on "Custom" to switch over.

You'll also see a version number next to the tabs (like v4.5). It's always good to make sure you're using the latest version to access all the newest features, but you can also switch to older versions if you prefer their sound.

Main Components of Custom Mode

Here are the essential parts of the Custom Mode screen:

- **Lyrics Box:** This is where your song's lyrics go. You have a lot of space to write, with character limits up to 3,000 for older versions and 5,000 for the latest ones.

- **Instrumental Toggle:** This is a simple on/off switch. Leave it off for songs with singing. Flip it on if you want to create a music-only track with no vocals.

- **Style Prompt Box:** This is where you describe the music you want. You can specify the genre, mood, instruments, and more. The character limit here has also increased, from around 200 characters in older versions to 1,000 in the latest, giving you more room to describe your sound. Next to the title, you'll see an orange button with a dice icon; this is the Style Prompt Enhancer. If you write a style, clicking this button will add more detail to it.

- **Title Box:** This is where you can give your song a name, up to 80 characters long. If you leave it blank, Suno will suggest a title for you based on your lyrics and style.

- **The "Create" Button:** This big, colorful button starts the music generation process. You can watch the progress of your song being made on the right side of the screen or find the finished tracks in your "Library."

Introduction to Lyrics Creation

Most popular songs follow a simple, predictable pattern. The most basic song structure is verse-chorus-verse. The verses tell the story, and the chorus is the repeating part with the main message.

Here is an example of a simple pop song about this very topic:

/* Song Title: "The Basic Structure of a Song" */

[Verse]
The verse tells a story
A new idea begins
Setting up the stage
For the part that spins

[Chorus]
The chorus is the hook
The part you know so well
It repeats the main line
A story it will tell

[Verse]
Another verse comes next
With different words to say
Building on the first part
In its own special way

[End]

The 3 Ways to Create Lyrics

In Custom Mode, you have three main ways to get lyrics for your song:

1. **Write or paste your own song:** This is the most direct method. You can type your own original lyrics directly into the "Lyrics Box." You can also paste in lyrics you've written elsewhere or generated with an external chatbot.

2. **Auto Mode:** If you press the "Auto" button above the lyrics box, you can just type a short idea or "seed" phrase. Suno will then use that idea to generate the full lyrics for you when you press the "Create" button. This option is best if you don't want to review or edit the lyrics before the song is made.

3. **Write Lyrics With Suno Help:** Suno offers two great options to help you write. The "By Line" button will generate lyrics one section at a time, allowing you to review and edit as you go. The "Full Song" button will generate the complete lyrics all at once, which you can then edit before making the music.

A quick note: Whether you use Suno or another chatbot to generate lyrics, it's always a good idea to review and edit the results. This is your chance to add your personal touch and make sure the words are just right for your song.

Creating Music with Style Prompts

This section is just a brief introduction to Style Prompts; we will cover them in much more detail in the next chapter. For now, think of a Style Prompt as your way of telling the AI musician what kind of music to play.

A basic style prompt usually has three attributes: **Mood**, **Genre**, and **Vocals**. You can write things like "Happy Pop" or "Sad Rock with female vocals." The only mandatory part is the genre.

And don't forget the **Prompt Enhancer** button (the orange button with the dice). If you're stuck, you can type a simple style like "Rock" and click this button to have Suno add more descriptive words for you.

Style Prompt Template

Here is a basic template you can use for simple style prompts:

[Mood] [Genre] [Vocals]

Here are five examples for popular genres:

- Upbeat Pop Female Vocals
- Melancholy Rock Male Vocals
- Energetic EDM Instrumental
- Soulful R&B Female Vocals
- Relaxed Hip-Hop Male Vocals

Advanced Topics

Suno has some very powerful features for more experienced users. The following topics are beyond the scope of this book, but it's good to know they exist for when you're ready to explore further:

- **Extend Songs:** You can make your songs much longer, up to 8 minutes.

- **Cover Songs:** You can take a song you've made and change its genre completely.

- **Upload audio:** You can upload an amateur audio recording and use Suno to turn it into a professional-sounding track.

- **Edit song:** Suno includes several editing tools, allowing you to replace sections, extend, crop, remove, and fade out parts of your song.

Case Study

Let's put this all together. Here are the lyrics for a song. Try pairing them with some of the different style prompts below to see how the same words can create totally different songs!

/* Song Title: "Going to the Disco" */

[Verse]
Flashing lights above
Feeling all the love
The beat is in my feet
Oh, this can't be beat

[Chorus]
Going to the disco
Dancing all night long
This is where I wanna go
Singing my favorite song

[Verse]
Spinning on the floor

Wanting more and more
The music feels so right
Under the disco light

[Bridge]
The world outside just fades away
I wish that I could always stay
Lost inside this groovy sound
Spinning 'round and 'round

[Chorus]
Going to the disco
Dancing all night long
This is where I wanna go
Singing my favorite song

Example Style Prompts:

1. Energetic Disco Female Vocals

2. Upbeat Pop Male Vocals

3. Driving Rock Female Vocals

4. Modern Country Male Vocals

5. Intense EDM Instrumental

Homework

- **Task 1:** Take the lyrics from the "Going to the Disco" case study and generate a song using at least two of the style prompts provided. Listen to the results and notice how different they sound.

- **Task 2:** Create your own song from scratch in Custom Mode! Write the lyrics, choose a style, and generate an enjoyable song. Save it to your "My Examples" playlist.

- **Task 3:** Go to the "Explore" section and find three songs that you find inspiring. Listen to their style and lyrics, and add them to your "Illustrative Songs" playlist for future reference.

Questions?

If you have questions about this chapter, ask the book's free companion chatbot. You can find the links in the Resources section of the book.

Chapter Summary

In this chapter, you moved beyond Simple Mode and got familiar with Custom Mode. You learned about its main components, like the separate boxes for lyrics and style, and discovered three different ways to get lyrics for your songs. We also had a brief look at how style prompts work to set the mood, genre, and vocals of your music.

Now that you know how to direct both the lyrics and the music, you have much more creative power. In the next chapter, we will really get into Style Prompts, learning all the tricks to describe the exact sound you want for your music.

Chapter 4: Learn to Compose Music with Style Prompts

In the last chapter, you learned your way around Custom Mode, separating lyrics from the music. Now it's time to become the musical director! The "Style Prompt" is your secret weapon, allowing you to tell Suno's AI precisely what kind of music you want. The better your Style Prompt, the more impressive and personalized your song will be.

Chapter Outline

- Defining Style Prompts
- Building Blocks of a Style Prompt
- Emphasis Techniques
- Style Prompt Templates
- Case Study
- Homework

Defining Style Prompts

Think of Style Prompts as your instructions to Suno's AI musician. You use words to describe the genre, mood, and instruments, and Suno translates those words into music.

Suno's Style Enhance button (the orange dice icon) is a fun way to get random, experimental ideas. But to really bring your own vision to life or create something authentic to a specific genre, you'll want to write your own prompts. Keep in mind that the prompt box has character limits, which have grown from around 200 characters in older versions to 1,000 in the latest ones.

It's important to remember that style prompts are suggestions, not commands. Suno is a creative partner. It considers your title, lyrics, and style prompt, then adds its own artistic interpretation. This can lead to wonderful surprises, but sometimes the result might not be exactly what you expected. If you're not satisfied, don't be afraid to experiment! Change a word or two in your prompt and try again.

The keywords and techniques in this chapter are a great starting point, but they are always evolving. We recommend starting with simple prompts and then gradually adding more details as you get comfortable. If you ever feel stuck, this chapter includes templates you can use to generate ideas.

Building Blocks of a Style Prompt

A well-made Style Prompt is built from several types of keywords. **Genre** is the only mandatory one, but the others give you much more control. You might not think you need them all at first, but as you get better, you'll use these keywords to make your songs richer and more detailed.

Genre
This is the main category of your music. (For a detailed list, see Appendix A).

- **Sample Keywords:** Pop, Rock, Hip Hop, EDM, Country
- **Example Prompts:**
    1. Acoustic Folk
    2. Classic Rock
    3. 90s Hip Hop

Mood
This sets the overall emotion of the song. (For a detailed list, see Appendix C).

- **Sample Keywords:** Happy, Sad, Energetic, Mysterious, Romantic

- **Example Prompts:**

    1. Energetic Pop

    2. Melancholy Piano Ballad

    3. Mysterious Electronic

Tempo
This controls the speed of the music. (For a detailed list, see Appendix D).

- **Sample Keywords:** Slow, Fast, Upbeat, Laid-back, Driving

- **Example Prompts:**

    1. Rock song with a driving beat

    2. Lofi Hip Hop with a laid-back tempo

    3. Upbeat Dance music

Vocals
This describes the singer's voice. (For a detailed list, see Appendix E).

- **Sample Keywords:** Male Vocal, Female Vocal, Raspy, Smooth, Powerful

- **Example Prompts:**

    1. Soul with a powerful female vocal

    2. Jazz with a smooth male vocal

    3. Punk Rock with an aggressive, raspy vocal

Instruments
This tells Suno what instruments to include. (For a detailed list, see Appendix F).

- **Sample Keywords:** Piano, Acoustic Guitar, Electric Guitar, Drums, Synth
- **Example Prompts:**
    1. Pop Ballad featuring piano and strings
    2. Hard Rock with heavy electric guitars and drums
    3. Synthwave featuring 80s synths

Sonic Textures
This describes the overall quality of the sound—is it thick, thin, clean, or hazy? (For a detailed list, see Appendix G).

- **Sample Keywords:** Atmospheric, Raw, Polished, Warm, Ethereal
- **Example Prompts:**
    1. Ambient music with an atmospheric and ethereal texture
    2. Garage Rock with a raw, gritty texture
    3. Pop song with a polished, clean sound

This refers to how the music is recorded and mixed. (For a detailed list, see Appendix H).

- **Sample Keywords:** Lo-fi, Hi-fi, Modern Production, Studio Recording, Radio-Friendly
- **Example Prompts:**
    1. Chillhop with Lo-fi Production
    2. Orchestral piece with a Hi-fi Studio Recording

3. Pop song with a Radio-Friendly Modern Production

Arrangement & Performance Style Keywords

This describes how the music is structured and performed. (For a detailed list, see Appendix I).

- **Sample Keywords:** Driving Beat, Groovy, Catchy Melody, Soaring Melody, Simple

- **Example Prompts:**

    1. Funk with a groovy, syncopated rhythm
    2. Pop anthem with a soaring, catchy melody
    3. Folk song with a simple, strummed acoustic guitar

Emphasis Techniques

Want Suno to pay extra attention to certain words? Use these emphasis techniques.

Brackets
Placing a word in [brackets] gives it more weight. Without brackets, Suno treats all words more or less equally.

- **Without Brackets:**

    1. Rock with heavy guitars
    2. Pop with a catchy chorus
    3. Folk with acoustic guitar

- **With Brackets:**

    1. Rock with [heavy guitars]

2. Pop with a [catchy chorus]

3. Folk with [acoustic guitar]

Capital Words

Using ALL CAPS also tells Suno to give a word more importance. You can even combine caps with brackets for maximum emphasis.

- **Without Caps:**

    1. Dark and mysterious electronic music

    2. Upbeat and fun pop song

    3. A song with powerful vocals

- **With Caps:**

    1. DARK and MYSTERIOUS electronic music

    2. UPBEAT and FUN pop song

    3. A song with [POWERFUL VOCALS]

Commas for Genre Influence

Commas play a big role in how Suno blends genres.

- **No Commas:** Suno treats this as one primary style, where earlier words influence the last one. For Indie Pop Rock, "Rock" is the main genre, with "Indie" and "Pop" as influences.

- **With Commas:** Suno will try to create a more equal blend or fusion of all the genres listed. Indie, Pop, Rock will result in a hybrid sound.

- **Without Commas:**

    1. Country Folk Blues

2. Synth Pop Wave

3. Jazz Soul Funk

- **With Commas:**

    1. Country, Folk, Blues

    2. Synth, Pop, Wave

    3. Jazz, Soul, Funk

Style Prompt Templates

Feeling overwhelmed by all the options? Don't worry! Here are two templates to make things easier.

Basic   Template
This is the simplest way to start. Just name a genre or subgenre.

- **Template:** [Genre/Subgenre]

- **Examples:**

    1. "Synthwave"

    2. "Country Ballad"

    3. "Hard Rock"

Advanced   Template
This template helps you express a more detailed musical vision. You don't need to use every parameter—just the ones you need. Only **Genre/Subgenre** is required. A good way to learn is to start with the genre and add one new parameter at a time.

- **Template:**
  Decade/Era, Genre/Subgenre*, Tempo, Mood, Vocals, Instruments, Sonic Textures, Production Techniques, Arrangement & Performance

- **Explanation of Parameters (Refer to Building Blocks for details):**
    - **Decade/Era:** The time period (e.g., 80s, 90s, modern).
    - **Genre/Subgenre*:** The main musical style (e.g., Pop, Rock, Indie Folk). This is required.
    - **Tempo:** The speed (e.g., fast, slow, upbeat).
    - **Mood:** The emotional feel (e.g., happy, sad, epic).
    - **Vocals:** The description of the singer's voice (e.g. male vocals, female vocals, etc.). Omit if the song is instrumental.
    - **Instruments:** Key instruments to include (e.g., piano, synths, electric guitar).
    - **Sonic Textures:** The overall sound quality (e.g., warm, raw, polished, atmospheric).
    - **Production Techniques:** The recording style (e.g., Lo-fi, Hi-fi, modern).
    - **Arrangement & Performance:** How the music is played (e.g., groovy, simple, catchy melody).
- **Examples:**
    1. 80s, Synth Pop, Upbeat Tempo, Fun Mood, Sultry Female Vocal, featuring synths and electronic drums, with a polished production.
    2. Modern, Indie Folk, Slow Tempo, Melancholy Mood, Male Vocal, featuring acoustic guitar and cello, with a raw, intimate sonic texture.

3. 90s, Grunge Rock, Driving Tempo, Angry Mood, Raspy Male Vocal, featuring distorted electric guitars, with a raw production and aggressive performance.

4. 70s, Funk, Groovy Tempo, Upbeat Mood, featuring a prominent bassline and horns, with a warm analog production.

5. Epic Orchestral, Fast Tempo, Heroic Mood, featuring strings and powerful brass, with a hi-fi studio recording and soaring melodies.

Case Study

Let's try transforming one song with five different styles using the Advanced Template.

/* Song Title: "Styling my Song" */

[Verse]
Got a feeling in my soul
Ready now to lose control
Gonna find the perfect sound
Spin the whole world right around

[Chorus]
Styling my song, a brand new way
Changing the vibe for a brighter day
With a different beat and a fresh new mood
This is my song, it's understood

[Verse]
From a whisper to a scream
Living out a crazy dream
Every note and every line
Making this music truly mine

[Bridge]
Rock and roll to a gentle beat
Something sad or something sweet
The power is in the words I choose
There's no way that I can lose

[Outro]

Genre Variations:

1. **Pop Version:** 2020s, Electropop, Upbeat Tempo, Joyful Mood, featuring synths and a punchy drum machine, with a polished, radio-friendly production.

2. **Rock Version:** 90s, Alternative Rock, Driving Tempo, Angsty Mood, featuring distorted electric guitars and loud drums, with a raw sonic texture.

3. **Country Version:** Modern, Country, Moderate Tempo, Heartfelt Mood, featuring acoustic guitar and fiddle, with a clear, warm production.

4. **Folk Version:** Indie Folk, Slow Tempo, Reflective Mood, featuring a fingerpicked acoustic guitar and a cello, with an intimate, raw production.

5. **EDM Version:** Energetic, House, Fast Tempo, Euphoric Mood, with a driving beat and a big bass drop, featuring a layered arrangement.

Homework

- **Task 1:** Take the lyrics for "Styling my Song" and generate a few versions in Suno using the style prompts from the case study. Listen to how much they change!

- **Task 2:** Now, create your dream song. Write some simple lyrics and then use the elements from this chapter to build a detailed Style Prompt. Generate it, save it to your "My Examples" playlist, and share it with a friend!

- **Task 3:** Go exploring on Suno and find 5 songs with interesting Style Prompts. Check what the creator wrote, listen to the result, and save the songs to your "Illustrative Songs" playlist.

- **Task 4:** Listen to this chapter's companion song in the book's official playlist: https://suno.com/playlist/0715eba6-45e6-4fe7-9893-

- 4b38aa7780cc

Questions?

If you have questions about this chapter, ask the book's free companion chatbot. You can find the links in the Resources section of the book.

Chapter Summary

Mastering Style Prompts is like learning a secret code to unlock Suno's full potential. In this chapter, you learned about the eight building blocks of a great prompt, from genre and mood to production and performance. You also saw how to add emphasis with brackets and capitalization, and how to blend genres using commas.

By using the right combination of keywords and techniques, you can guide the AI to create songs that sound exactly how you imagine them. In the next chapter, we'll look at "Metatags"—the tools that let you control specific sections of your song, giving you even more precision.

Chapter 5: Learn to Create Lyrics with Metatags

In the last chapter, you became a musical director by learning to use Style Prompts. Now, it's time to get even more detailed. This chapter is all about "Metatags"—your secret weapon for shaping specific parts of your songs. Think of it as giving your AI musician a musical roadmap, guiding its choices with more precision.

Chapter Outline

- Defining Metatags
- Structural Metatags
- Basic Song Sections
- Transitional & Instrumental Sections
- Ending Tags
- Instrumental Performance
- Vocal Delivery
- Template to Create Lyrics
- Case Study
- Homework

Defining Metatags

Metatags are special instructions that you place inside your lyrics to guide Suno's AI. They are keywords enclosed in square brackets [] that tell Suno how to arrange the music, what instruments to use, and how to deliver the vocals. The best part? Suno reads them as commands but doesn't actually sing the words in the brackets.

Metatags only work in **Custom Mode**, inside the **lyrics box**. This box has generous character limits (up to 3,000 for older versions and 5,000 for the latest), so you have plenty of room to write.

Remember, metatags are suggestions. Suno is a creative partner that considers your title, lyrics, and style prompt, then adds its own artistic flair. This can lead to amazing surprises! If the result isn't quite what you wanted, don't be afraid to experiment.

You can even choose to use no metatags at all. By leaving them out, you give Suno complete control over the song's structure. Sometimes this produces fantastic, unexpected results, and other times... not so much. The fewer metatags you use, the more control Suno has.

The world of metatags is always growing. We'll cover the main ones here, but it's a great idea to start with the basics to avoid getting overwhelmed. If you ever feel stuck creating lyrics, this chapter includes a template you can use with an external chatbot to get you started.

Structural Metatags

Structural metatags are keywords that help you organize the different parts of your song, like the verse, chorus, and bridge. Song structures can vary a lot depending on the genre, but we'll look at the most common building blocks. For a more detailed list of tags, you can always check Appendix B.

Basic Song Sections

These are the most common parts of a song. The purpose of using different sections is to provide variety and keep the listener engaged.

- **[Intro]**: The beginning of the song that sets the mood.

- **[Verse] / [Verse 1] / [Verse 2]**: The parts that tell the story.
- **[Pre-Chorus]**: A section that builds excitement and leads into the chorus.
- **[Chorus]**: The main, repeated part of the song with the core message.
- **[Post-Chorus]**: A short section that can follow a chorus to add extra punch or transition smoothly.
- **[Bridge]**: A section that sounds different and provides an emotional shift.
- **[Outro]**: The end of the song that brings it to a satisfying close.

Typical Song Template

Real songs can have many verses and choruses, but a common and effective structure you can use as a template is:

[Intro] - [Verse] - [Pre-Chorus] - [Chorus] - [Post-Chorus] - [Bridge] - [Outro]

Example

Here is a short pop song that uses a simple structure.

/* Song Title: "City Lights" */

[Intro]

[Verse]
Streetlights glowing, night comes alive
In this busy city, we all strive
A million stories in the air
Chasing dreams without a care

[Chorus]
Oh, the city lights, they shine so bright

Guiding us all through the night
In this concrete jungle, we feel the beat
Dancing to the rhythm of the street

[Bridge]
Moments pass in a neon haze
Lost inside these city ways
But in the crowd, I see your face
A quiet moment, a special place

[Chorus]
Oh, the city lights, they shine so bright
Guiding us all through the night
In this concrete jungle, we feel the beat
Dancing to the rhythm of the street

[Outro]

Transitional & Instrumental Sections

These are sections, often without vocals, that create a sense of space, build anticipation, or provide a moment of contrast. It's best to place these between main sections, like after a chorus or before a bridge.

- **[Interlude]**: A short musical piece that connects two larger sections.

- **[Break] / [Musical Break]**: A short pause where some instruments might drop out.

- **[Transition]**: A tag to help signal a change from one part of the song to another.

- **[Instrumental]**: Creates a section with only instruments.

- **[Instrumental Break]**: A short instrumental pause in a song that has vocals.

- **[Instrumental Interlude]**: A longer instrumental section.
- **[Solo] / ['Instrument' Solo]**: A moment for one instrument to be featured (e.g., [Guitar Solo]).

For a list of specific instruments you can call for a solo, see Appendix B.

Ending Tags

How you end your song is just as important as how you begin it. These tags give you control over the final moments.

- **[End]**: Use this for a clear, abrupt ending. The music will just stop.
- **[Fade Out] / [Fade to End]**: These tags tell Suno to gradually decrease the volume for a smooth close.
- **[Finale] / [Big Finish]**: These suggest a grand, climactic ending.

Instrumental Performance

You can get even more specific by telling Suno *how* to play an instrument.

For example:

- [Fingerstyle Guitar Solo]
- [Synth Arpeggio]
- [Acoustic Guitar Strumming]

For a more detailed list of performance styles, refer to Appendix B.

Vocal Delivery

With metatags, you can control how the lyrics are sung or spoken in any section of your song.

Vocal Type / Gender
This is where you can specify who is singing.

- **[Male Vocals] / [Female Vocals]**: Specifies a male or female singer.

- **[Man] / [Woman] / [Boy] / [Girl]**: More specific tags for vocal character.

Styling Vocals

By default, Suno sings the lyrics. But you can use these tags to have parts spoken for dramatic effect.

- **[Spoken Word]**: For general spoken sections, like narration.

- **[Shout] / [Scream]**: For loud, emphatic spoken parts.

- **[Poetry]**: For a more dramatic, poetic delivery.

Vocal Grouping & Harmonies
Want more than one voice? Use these tags.

- **[Choir] / [Gospel Choir]**: A group of singers performing together.

- **[Backup Vocals]**: Adds supporting voices behind the main singer.

- **[Vocal Harmony]**: Creates additional vocal lines that sound pleasing with the melody.

Vocal Tone & Quality
This helps set the emotional feel of the singing.

- **[Soft Vocals]**: For a gentle, delicate performance.
- **[Powerful Vocals]**: For a strong, commanding vocal delivery.
- **[Melancholy Vocals]**: For a sad, thoughtful vocal tone.

Vocal **Effects**
Add some sonic spice to your vocals with effects.

- **[Vocaloid]**: A robotic or synthesized voice.
- **[Autotune]**: The iconic pitch-correction effect.
- **[Echo]**: Creates repeating, decaying vocal sounds.

You can combine vocal tags with structural tags to get very specific. Here are a few examples:

1. [Verse 1][Male Vocals][Soft Vocals]
   The city sleeps, but I'm awake...

2. [Chorus][Female Vocals][Powerful Vocals][Vocal Harmony]
   We're gonna rise up, and seize the day...

3. [Bridge][Spoken Word][Whisper]
   And in the silence, all I heard was your name...

Templates to Create Lyrics

If you need help coming up with lyrics, you can use a chatbot like ChatGPT. Here are some templates to get you started.

Basic Template:
Create a [genre/subgenre] song lyrics about [Theme/Scenario/Story].

Advanced Template:
Create a [genre/subgenre] song lyrics about [Theme/Scenario/Story]. Adjust the lyrics flow/delivery for the chosen genre. Use this [Structure] for this song. Use 'n' (short/long) lines per section. Format the output for Suno.

Parameters:

- **[genre/subgenre]**: The style of music (e.g., Pop, Rock, Country).

- **[Theme/Topic/Scenario]**: What the song is about (e.g., a breakup, a summer road trip).

- **[Structure]**: The song structure you want (e.g., Verse-Chorus-Verse).

- **n**: The number of lines you want per section.

Example Prompts:

1. Create a Rock song lyrics about overcoming a challenge. Use a Verse-Chorus-Verse-Bridge-Chorus structure. Use 4 short lines per section. Format the output for Suno.

2. Create a Country song lyrics about missing home. Use an Intro-Verse-Chorus structure. Use 8 long lines per section. Format the output for Suno.

3. Create an EDM song lyrics about a massive party. Use a Verse-Build-Chorus-Drop structure. Use 4 short lines per section. Format the output for Suno.

Note: Always review and edit lyrics generated by a chatbot to make sure they fit your artistic vision!

Case Study

Let's see how adding metatags can transform a simple song.

Base Song Example
Here are the base lyrics for a pop song.

/* Song Title: "You Inspire Me" */

[Verse]
Lost in the noise, I couldn't see
Just what my heart was telling me
You came along, a guiding light
And made everything feel so right

[Chorus]
You inspire me to be so strong
You're the melody in my life's song
With you beside me, I can fly
Reaching for a brand new sky

[Verse]
I was afraid to take a chance
Stuck inside a lonely dance
You took my hand and pulled me through
Showed me a world completely new

[Bridge]
Every word you say to me
Helps my spirit to break free
I'll follow you to any place
With a smile upon my face

[Chorus]
You inspire me to be so strong
You're the melody in my life's song
With you beside me, I can fly
Reaching for a brand new sky

[End]

Add a Spoken Word Introduction
Let's add a dramatic introduction.

[Intro]

[Spoken Word]
I was searching for a reason, a spark in the dark. And then, there was you.

[Verse]...

Add a Transitional Instrumental Section
Let's place a short instrumental after the first verse to build emotion.

...
[Verse]
...
[Instrumental]
[Bridge]
...

Add a Choir to the Chorus
Let's make the chorus sound bigger and more epic with a choir.

...
[Chorus][Choir]
You inspire me to be so strong

...
[Chorus][Choir]
You inspire me to be so strong
...

Add Male and Female Voices
Let's have a male voice sing the verses and a female voice lead the chorus for a duet feel.

...
[Verse][Male Voice]
Lost in the noise, I couldn't see
...
[Chorus][Choir][Female Voice]
You inspire me to be so strong
...
[Verse][Male Voice]
I was afraid to take a chance
...

Change the Ending
Instead of an abrupt stop, let's have the song fade out nicely.

...
[Fade to End]

Final Song
Here is the complete song with all our new metatags.

/* Song Title: "You Inspire Me" */

[Intro]

[Spoken Word]
I was searching for a reason, a spark in the dark. And then, there was you.

[Verse][Male Voice]
Lost in the noise, I couldn't see
Just what my heart was telling me
You came along, a guiding light
And made everything feel so right

[Instrumental]

[Chorus][Choir][Female Voice]
You inspire me to be so strong
You're the melody in my life's song

With you beside me, I can fly
Reaching for a brand new sky

[Verse][Male Voice]
I was afraid to take a chance
Stuck inside a lonely dance
You took my hand and pulled me through
Showed me a world completely new

[Bridge]
Every word you say to me
Helps my spirit to break free
I'll follow you to any place
With a smile upon my face

[Chorus][Choir][Female Voice]
You inspire me to be so strong
You're the melody in my life's song
With you beside me, I can fly
Reaching for a brand new sky

[Fade to End]

Suggested Style Prompt:
"Uplifting Pop Ballad, modern production, powerful vocals, with piano and soaring strings"

Homework

- **Task 1:** Take the final version of "You Inspire Me" from the case study and generate it in Suno. Listen to how the different metatags affect the final song.

- **Task 2:** Create a brand new song that you want to share with the world. Write your own lyrics and use metatags to add effects, change instruments, and control the vocals. Save it to your "My Songs" playlist.

- **Task 3:** Find three songs on Suno that use metatags in cool or creative ways. Save them to your "Illustrative Songs" playlist for future reference.

- **Task 4:** Listen to this chapter's companion song in the book's official playlist: https://suno.com/playlist/0715eba6-45e6-4fe7-9893-4b38aa7780cc

Questions?

If you have questions about this chapter, ask the book's free companion chatbot. You can find the links in the Resources section of the book.

Chapter Summary

You've just learned one of the most powerful features in Suno: Metatags. In this chapter, you saw how these simple bracketed commands can structure your songs, call for specific instruments, and control everything about the vocal performance. From basic song sections to advanced vocal effects, you now have the tools to act as a producer for your AI-generated music.

Now that you can direct the arrangement, what's next? In the following chapter, we'll look at advanced lyric formatting techniques that will give you even more control over Suno's vocal delivery. Get ready to add even more character and personality to your songs

Chapter 6: Personalize Songs with Lyric Formatters

You've learned the basics of lyrics and style prompts, and you've even directed the band with metatags. Now it's time to add some real personality to your songs by unlocking the power of **lyric formatters**. These are the tools that give you detailed control over *how* Suno's AI delivers your lyrics, shaping the rhythm, emotion, and unique vocal flourishes that will make your music stand out.

Chapter Outline

- Definition of Lyric Formatters
- Punctuation for Pauses and Phrasing
- Line Breaks for Rhythmic Pauses
- Capitalization for Emphasis
- Asterisks for Whispers and Echoes
- Parentheses for Ad-Libs and Asides
- Vocal Metatags for Flow
- Case Study: All Lyric Formatters in Action
- Homework

Definition of Lyric Formatters

Lyric formatters are punctuation marks, characters, or metatags you use *within your lyrics* to influence how Suno sings them. They can shape rhythm, emphasis, vocal style, pauses, and overall expression.

These tools work their magic primarily in **Custom Mode**, inside the lyrics box. The main types we'll cover are Punctuation, Line Breaks, Capitalization, Parentheses (for ad-libs), Asterisks, and special Vocal Metatags [].

Remember, these formatters are suggestions. Suno is a bit of a free spirit! It will interpret your instructions in the context of the whole song and its own artistic choices. Experimentation is key to getting the sound you're looking for.

One important rule: forget your grammar lessons! In Suno, punctuation is used for musical delivery, not correctness. Avoid putting a period at the end of every line unless you *want* a full stop in the music. The same goes for capitalization and other formatters—use them with a musical purpose in mind.

Punctuation for Pauses and Phrasing

Punctuation marks are your tools for creating intentional pauses, guiding the musical phrasing and vocal delivery.

- **Period (.)**: Creates the strongest pause, like a full stop in a sentence.
- **Comma (,)**: A shorter pause, like taking a quick breath.
- **Dash (-)**: Can create a dramatic break or a thoughtful pause.
- **Ellipsis (...)**: Suggests trailing off, hesitation, or suspense.

Example: "Love is Heaven" (Pop Style)

Version 1: No Punctuation	Version 2: With Punctuation
You walked in my world	You walked in... a new world for me.
You changed everything I see	You changed everything, I see
My heart beats a brand new sound	My heart beats a new sound- a new song
Love is heaven when you're around	Love is heaven, when you are around.

Notice how the punctuation in Version 2 changes the flow. The ellipsis creates suspense, the commas add breaths, and the periods create full stops, making the delivery feel more deliberate and emotional.

Line Breaks for Rhythmic Pauses

Inserting blank lines between your lyric lines creates musical rests, or silences. This can affect the pacing of the song, add a little tension, or give the listener a moment to breathe.

Example: "I Got a Salary Raise" (Pop Style)

Version 1: Consecutive Lines	Version 2: With Line Breaks
Check my bank account now	Check my bank account now
A brand new number appears	
No more instant ramen	A brand new number appears
I'm over all my fears	
	No more instant ramen
	I'm over all my fears

The blank lines in Version 2 will create short, rhythmic pauses in the song, giving it a more staccato and impactful feel compared to the continuous flow of Version 1.

Capitalization for Emphasis

Capitalization is your tool for controlling the vocal dynamics—how loud or soft certain words are sung.

- **Normal Sentence case:** Creates a standard, neutral vocal delivery.
- **Selective Word(s) CAPS:** Adds stress to specific words, making them stand out with more intensity.
- **ALL CAPS PHRASE:** Signals a much louder delivery, like shouting, perfect for high-energy moments.

Example: "I Got a Job" (Pop Style)

Version 1: Normal Case Version 2: With Emphasis

Version 1	Version 2
I finally got the call today	I finally got the call today
Everything will be okay	Everything is GONNA be okay
I'm ready to start a new life	I'm ready to start a NEW life
I'm gonna celebrate tonight	I'M GONNA CELEBRATE ALL NIGHT LONG!

In Version 2, the capitalized words will be sung with more power. "GONNA" and "NEW" get a little punch, while the final line will be delivered with maximum energy.

Asterisks for Whispers and Echoes

Placing *asterisks* around a word or phrase can *suggest* that Suno deliver it more softly, like a whisper, or with a slight echo effect. This effect can be subtle and sometimes inconsistent, so experimentation is key!

Example: "I Won The Lottery" (Pop Style)

Version 1: Standard Text	Version 2: With Asterisks
I can't believe the numbers I see	I can't believe the numbers I see
Is this really happening to me	*Is this really happening to me*
My whole world is about to change	My whole world is about to change
Life will never feel the same again	*Life will feel brand new again*

Listen closely when you generate Version 2. The phrases in asterisks might sound softer, more distant, or have a hint of reverb, adding a dreamy quality to the song.

Parentheses for Ad-Libs and Asides

Ad-libs are those "oohs," "yeahs," or short phrases that add flavor and energy to a song. In Suno, you use (parentheses) to create them. They can act as background vocals, call-and-response elements, or little comments from the singer.

- **Start of a line:** Can create anticipation.
- **Middle of a line:** Can act as an interjection or response.
- **End of a line:** Can sound like an echo or backing vocal.

Example: "I Won The Lottery" (Pop Style)

Version 1: No Ad-Libs	Version 2: With Ad-Libs
I won the lottery today	(Oh yeah) I won the lottery today
I'm gonna do things my way	I'm gonna do things (my way)
No more working nine to five	No more (never more!) working nine to five
I feel so alive	I feel so alive (so alive)

The ad-libs in Version 2 add a whole new layer of excitement and energy, making the song feel more like a live performance.

Vocal Metatags for Flow

While the formatters above are subtle hints, metatags ([square brackets]) give Suno more direct instructions for vocal style. (For a detailed list, see Appendix B).

- **Vocal Delivery Style:** Change from singing to other deliveries.
    - [Spoken Word], [Rap Vocals], [Whispered Vocals], [Screaming], [Scat Singing]

- **Musical Articulation for Vocals:** How notes are sung.
    - [Staccato Vocals] (short, detached notes), [Legato Vocals] (smooth, connected notes).
- **Vocal Arrangement/Grouping:** For vocal-only parts or groups.
    - [Acapella], [Vocal Percussion], [Choir], [Backup Vocals]
- **Vocal Effects:** Apply processing to the voice.
    - [Autotune], [Vocoder], [Reverb Vocals]

Example: "The City I Love"

Version 1: Basic Structure	Version 2: With Vocal Metatags
[Verse]	[Verse][Spoken Word]
The city breathes at night	The city breathes at night
A symphony of sound and light	A symphony of sound and light
Each street a different story	Each street a different story
In all its grit and glory	In all its grit and glory
[Chorus]	[Chorus][Powerful Vocals]
This is the city I love	This is the city I love
The energy from up above	The energy from up above
It never sleeps it never ends	It never sleeps it never ends
A million strangers become friends	A million strangers become friends
[Verse]	[Verse][Rap Vocals]
The subway rumbles down below	The subway rumbles down below
People rushing to and fro	People rushing to and fro
A pulse that's fast a beat that's deep	A pulse that's fast a beat that's deep
While the quiet alleys sleep	While the quiet alleys sleep

In Version 2, the first verse becomes a narrated intro, the chorus is sung with power, and the second verse is delivered as a rap, completely changing the song's dynamic journey.

Case Study: All Lyric Formatters in Action

Let's combine all these tools to see how they can transform a song.

Example: "Formatting My Flow" (Pop Style)

Version 1: Standard Lyrics	Version 2: With Lyric Formatters
[Verse]	**[Verse][Spoken Word]**
This is just a simple line	This is just a simple line...
I'll make the rhythm mine	I'll make the rhythm ALL mine.
Each word a different beat	Each word, a different beat
A sonic, special treat	A *sonic, special treat*.
[Chorus]	**[Chorus][Powerful Vocals]**
I'm formatting my flow	I'm formatting my flow (My flow)
Putting on a special show	Putting on a SPECIAL show
The music's in control	The music's in control (Oh yeah)
It's taking over my soul	It's taking over my SOUL!
[Verse]	**[Verse][Rap Vocals]**
Punctuation is the key	Punctuation is the key,
To set the vocals free	
	to set the vocals free.
A comma makes a pause	A comma makes a pause,
I'm breaking all the laws	
	I'm breakin' all the LAWS.
[Bridge]	**[Bridge][Whispered Vocals]**
Listen closely to the sound	*Listen closely to the sound*
Magic's all around	*magic's all around*

Every little tiny change	Every... little... tiny... change
Makes the song rearrange	Makes the song rearrange.
[Chorus]	**[Chorus][Choir][Autotune]**
I'm formatting my flow	I'm formatting my flow (My flow)
Putting on a special show	Putting on a SPECIAL show
The music's in control	The music's in control (Oh yeah)
It's taking over my soul	It's taking over my SOUL!

Version 2 is a completely different experience. It starts with a spoken word intro, builds energy with capitalized words and ad-libs in the chorus, experiments with rhythm using line breaks in the rap verse, and creates a dramatic, whispered bridge. We suggest you test both versions in Suno to hear the difference for yourself!

Homework

- **Task 1:** Generate the two versions of "Formatting My Flow" from the Case Study. Listen carefully and evaluate the impact the lyric formatters have on the final song.

- **Task 2:** Write lyrics for a personal song. Experiment with your favorite formatting techniques from this chapter. Apply punctuation, ad-libs, and capitalization to make it your own. Save the result to your "My Songs" playlist.

- **Task 3:** Search on Suno for songs that use lyric formatters in a smart or creative way. Add a few to your "Illustrative Songs" playlist for future inspiration.

- **Task 4:** Listen to this chapter's companion song in the book's official playlist: https://suno.com/playlist/0715eba6-45e6-4fe7-9893-4b38aa7780cc

Questions?

If you have questions about this chapter, ask the book's free companion chatbot. You can find the links in the Resources section of the book.

Chapter Summary

You've just learned how to be a vocal director for your Suno songs! In this chapter, we looked at how lyric formatters like punctuation, capitalization, and parentheses can add personality and expression to your music. You saw how these simple tools can control rhythm, create emphasis, and add vocal flair.

You now have a powerful set of tools to make your music even more dynamic and unique. In the next chapter, we'll learn some basic music theory concepts and see how they can help you create even more catchy and effective songs.

Chapter 7: How to Create Catchy Songs

In the last chapter, you learned how to add personality to your songs using lyric formatters. Now, let's go for the gold: making songs that get stuck in people's heads! While there's no magic formula for a guaranteed hit, there are proven ingredients that make a song "catchy." This chapter will show you what those ingredients are and how you can use them in Suno to create your own unforgettable tunes.

Chapter Outline

- Unlocking the Psychology of Catchiness
- The Repetitive Metatags Review
- The Seven Key Ingredients of Catchiness
- Balancing the Catchy Elements
- Making it Catchy in Suno: Practical Tips
- Catchy Prompt Templates (for Suno)
- Case Study: Taking "I Won the Lottery" from Basic to Super-Catchy (Trap Style)
- Homework

Unlocking the Psychology of Catchiness

Ever had a song stuck in your head on a loop? That's the power of catchiness. It's not just random; there's a science to why some songs are so memorable.

The psychology of catchiness boils down to a few key ideas:

- **The Earworm Effect:** This is when a part of a song, usually the chorus, repeats in your mind over and over.

- **The Sing-Along Factor:** Catchy songs are often easy to sing, making you want to join in.

- **Emotional Resonance:** The song connects with a feeling you understand, whether it's joy, sadness, or excitement.

The Science Behind Catchiness

- **Pattern Recognition**
  Our brains are wired to seek and recognize patterns. Simple, repetitive melodies are easy for the brain to process, which makes them instantly enjoyable.

- **Melodic Simplicity = Musical Candy**
  Catchy hooks often use repetition and simplicity. This makes them feel familiar quickly, like musical "candy" for our minds.

- **Dopamine Release: The Reward System**
  When we hear a melody we like, our brain releases dopamine, the same "addictive" chemical associated with pleasure and reward. This reinforces the desire to hear the song again.

- **Emotional Memory**
  That dopamine boost also helps anchor the song to our emotions and memories. This emotional connection makes the song more memorable—and harder to forget.

- **The Repeat/Replay Effect**
  The combination of pattern recognition, dopamine, and emotional memory creates a loop: we enjoy the song, feel good, remember it emotionally, and want to hear it again.

"Normal" Songs vs. "Catchy" Songs

- **"Normal" Songs:** Artists often create songs to express a unique artistic vision, share a personal experience, or appeal to a specific group of listeners. These songs can be complex and deeply meaningful but aren't always designed to get stuck in everyone's head.
- **"Catchy" Songs:** These songs are often built specifically for memorability and broad appeal. They typically feature simple structures, powerful emotional hooks, and lots of repetition to make them instantly recognizable.

Note: Of course, not all catchy songs become massive hits, and many popular chart-topping songs have complex, artistic structures. But understanding the principles of catchiness gives you a powerful tool for your songwriting toolkit.

The Repetitive Metatags Review

Repetition is the king of catchiness. In Suno, you can use specific metatags to define the parts of your song you want to be the most repetitive and memorable.

- **[Chorus]**: This is the main, repeated section. It should contain the core message and the most memorable melody of your song. You'll want to use this tag multiple times.
- **[Hook] / [Catchy Hook]**: The hook is the single most memorable part of your song. It can be a short lyrical phrase or an instrumental riff. Using these tags tells Suno to make this part extra "sticky."
- **[Refrain]**: This is a line or phrase that repeats, but it's usually part of a verse, not a standalone section like a

chorus. It helps to reinforce an idea without stopping the story.

Repetition also applies to the music itself. You can ask for a "repetitive synth riff" or a "simple, repeating drum pattern" in your Style Prompt to make the music as catchy as the lyrics.

The Seven Key Ingredients of Catchiness

Here are the seven key elements that make a song catchy.

1. **Simplicity**: Keep melodies, lyrics, and song structures easy to follow. The song "Twist and Shout" by The Beatles is a great example; its melody and chords are incredibly simple, making it easy for anyone to sing along.
2. **Repetition**: Strategically repeat your most important ideas. In "Uptown Funk" by Mark Ronson ft. Bruno Mars, the phrase "Uptown funk you up" is repeated so many times that it's impossible to forget.
3. **Familiarity**: Use patterns that feel comfortable and recognizable. The Weeknd's "Blinding Lights" uses a drum beat and synth sound that is instantly familiar to anyone who's heard 80s pop music, making it feel both new and classic at the same time.
4. **Predictability**: Build songs that listeners can anticipate. Predictability is about what comes *next*. When you hear the first part of a chorus, your brain can often predict how it will end. Justin Timberlake's "Can't Stop the Feeling!" has a very predictable pop structure, which makes it feel satisfying and easy to follow.
5. **Surprise**: Introduce brief, unexpected changes to keep things interesting. A great example is the pause before the chorus in "Good as Hell" by Lizzo. That moment of

silence makes the return of the music even more impactful.

6. **Novelty**: While the core of the song might be familiar, adding a new or different section, like a bridge or a rap verse, provides variation. Surprise is a short interruption; novelty is a longer change of scenery. The spoken-word part "Shake it like a Polaroid picture" in OutKast's "Hey Ya!" is a perfect example of a novel section that became iconic.

7. **Emotional Connection**: Tap into universal feelings. Adele's "Someone Like You" is a masterclass in this. The lyrics about lost love and the emotional vocal delivery connect with a feeling that almost everyone has experienced.

Balancing the Catchy Elements

The secret to a great catchy song is balance.

- **Simplicity vs. Complexity:** Too simple is boring, but too complex is hard to follow. A good guideline is to aim for about **80% simplicity and 20% complexity**. For example, you could have simple verses with just a few instruments and four short lines, but then add a more complex pre-chorus that builds excitement.

- **Familiarity vs. Novelty:** Too familiar sounds generic, but too novel can feel weird. Try grounding your song in about **80% familiar elements** (like a standard pop structure) and then introduce **20% novel elements** (like a surprising sound effect or a unique bridge section).

- **Predictability vs. Surprise:** Too predictable is monotonous, but too many surprises can be confusing. Keep the overall structure about **80% predictable**, which leaves **20% room for surprises**, like adding an instrumental break where a verse would normally be.

- **Repetition vs. Variation:** Too much repetition is annoying, but too little makes a song forgettable. A good rule is to **repeat your chorus or main hook at least 3-6 times**. You can then provide variation in the verses and bridge to keep the song moving forward. For example, a structure like Verse-Chorus-Verse-Chorus-Bridge-Chorus-Chorus-End gives you plenty of repetition.

Tips to Making it Catchy in Suno

Here's how to apply these ideas directly in Suno.

A. On the Lyrics Side (Using Metatags and Formatters):

- Define your catchy sections with [Chorus] and [Hook]. Often, a [Hook] works well right after a [Chorus], and a [Refrain] can be used at the end of [Verse] sections to reinforce an idea.

- Write deliberately repetitive phrases in your chorus and hook lyrics.

- Use lyric formatters for impact: create surprise pauses with **punctuation**, emphasize hook words with **CAPITALIZATION**, and add call-and-response energy with **parenthetical ad-libs (Yeah!)**.

B. On the Style Prompt Side:

- **Simplicity:** Don't overstuff your prompt. Focus on the core genre and mood.

- **Familiarity:** Clearly state the main genre (e.g., "Pop," "Country," "Rock").

- **Repetition/Hooks:** Explicitly ask for what you want: "catchy hook," "memorable melody," "repetitive synth riff."

- **Surprise/Novelty:** You can suggest things like "unexpected instrumental break" or "a brief spoken word interlude."

- **Emotional Tone:** Use strong mood words like "joyful," "heartbreaking," or "energetic."

Example Style Prompts for Catchiness:

1. **Pop:** Energetic Pop, with a very catchy vocal hook and a memorable synth melody.

2. **Rock:** Anthemic Rock, with a powerful, repetitive guitar riff and a simple, sing-along chorus.

3. **Hip-Hop:** Lofi Hip-Hop, with a simple, looping piano melody and a catchy, laid-back vocal hook.

4. **Country:** Upbeat Country, with a super catchy fiddle hook and a simple, storytelling chorus.

5. **EDM:** Euphoric Dance music, with a simple, repetitive synth lead and an unforgettable vocal chop hook.

Catchy Prompt Templates

A. Template to Generate Catchy Lyrics:

- **Basic Template:**
  Create the lyrics for a [genre/subgenre] song about [theme/scenario/story], with a very repetitive and

simple chorus and, if apply, a hook and refrain to reinforce the main message. Structure: [e.g., Verse-Chorus-Verse-Chorus-Bridge-Chorus] with 4 short lines per section. Emphasize [emotional connection]

- **Advanced Template:**
  Create the lyrics for a [genre/subgenre] song about [theme/scenario/story], with a very repetitive and simple chorus and, if apply, a hook and refrain to reinforce the main message. Use simple language, a clear [AABB or ABAB] rhyme scheme for the verses. Use the structure: [structure]. Use 4 short lines per section. Emphasize [emotional connection].

- **Note**: Feel free to modify this template prompt to adapt it to your own artistic needs.

B. Template to Generate Catchy Music:

- **Basic Style Prompt for Catchiness:**
  [Genre/Subgenre], [Main Catchy Element]

  - **Examples:**
    1. Dance Pop, catchy synth hook
    2. Indie Rock, repetitive bassline
    3. Country Pop, memorable vocal hook
    4. House Music, simple piano melody
    5. Trap, catchy 808 pattern

- **Advanced Style Prompt for Catchiness:** This template adds a special mandatory element: the **Main Catchy Element**. This tells Suno the most important "sticky" part you want in the music.

Decade/Era, Genre/Subgenre*, **Main Catchy Element***, Tempo, Mood, Instruments, Vocal Style, Sonic Textures, Production Techniques, Arrangement & Performance

Note: Feel free to modify this template prompt to adapt it to your own artistic needs.

- **Examples:**
    1. 2020s, **Pop Rock, extremely catchy guitar riff**, Upbeat, Energetic, Male Vocal
    2. 80s, **Synthwave, memorable and simple synth melody**, Driving Beat, Nostalgic
    3. **Trap, highly repetitive and catchy hi-hat pattern**, 140 BPM, Hype, Autotuned Male Rap
    4. **Disco, very groovy and repetitive bassline**, 120 BPM, Funky, Female Vocal with Harmonies
    5. **Folk Pop, simple and catchy acoustic guitar strumming pattern**, Hopeful, Duet Vocals

Case Study: Taking "I Won the Lottery" from Basic to Super-Catchy

Part 1: The Basic Version

- **Lyrics:**
  [Verse]
  Looked at the ticket in my hand

Suddenly I understand
All the numbers lined up right
Everything changed overnight

[Chorus]
I won the lottery
Now my life is free
This feels like a dream
A happy, joyful scene

[Verse]
No more work, no more debt
This is the best day yet
Gonna travel 'round the world
My new story has unfurled

- **Style Prompt:** Trap beat

- **Analysis:** This is a good start. It will sound like a trap song, but it might not be very memorable yet.

Part 2: Adding Novelty & Structure

- **Modify Lyrics:** Let's add an [Intro], [Bridge], and [Outro] to give the song a more complete journey.

- **Schema:** [Intro] - [Verse] - [Chorus] - [Verse] - [Bridge] - [Chorus] - [Outro]

- **New Bridge Lyrics:**
  [Bridge]
  Used to worry, used to stress
  My whole life was just a mess
  But now I'm flying high above
  Filled with so much peace and love

- **Analysis:** The song feels more complete now, with a new section that adds emotional contrast.

Part 3: Injecting Repetition & a Stronger Hook

- **Modify Lyrics:** Let's make the chorus super simple and add a hook right after it. We'll also repeat the chorus more often.

- **Schema:** [Intro] - [Verse] - [Chorus] - [Hook] - [Verse] - [Bridge] - [Chorus] - [Hook] - [Chorus] - [Hook] - [Outro]

- **New Chorus and Hook:**
  [Chorus]
  Big money, yeah, big money, yeah
  Big money, got that big money, yeah
  Big money, yeah, big money, yeah
  Big money, now I'm so carefree

  [Hook]
  (Money, money, money, yeah!)

- **Analysis:** The simple, repetitive chorus and the shout-out hook are much more likely to get stuck in a listener's head.

Part 4: Introducing Surprise

- **Modify Lyrics/Style:** Let's add a surprise element. We can add a [Record Scratch] metatag right before the last chorus to create a sudden pause.

- **Schema:** ...[Bridge] - [Record Scratch] - [Chorus] - [Hook]...

- **Analysis:** This short, unexpected sound will grab the listener's attention and make the final chorus hit even harder.

Part 5: Enhancing the Style Prompt for Maximum Catchiness

- **Refined Style Prompt:** Modern Trap, extremely catchy and simple synth hook melody, 150 BPM, Hype mood, autotuned male rap vocal with ad-libs, driving 808 bass, crisp and repetitive hi-hats, a brief silent break before the last chorus

- **Analysis:** This prompt is much more specific. It asks for a catchy melody, sets a hype mood, defines the vocal style, and even requests the surprise element we planned.

Part 6: The Final Catchy Song

/* Song Title: "I Won the Lottery" */

[Intro]

[Record Scratch]

[Spoken Word]

I won the lottery, this is my story

[Verse]
Looked at the ticket in my hand
Suddenly I understand
All the numbers lined up right
Everything changed overnight

[Chorus]
Big money, yeah, big money, yeah
Big money, got that big money, yeah
Big money, yeah, big money, yeah
Big money, now I'm so carefree

[Hook]
(Money, money, money, yeah!)

[Verse]
No more work, no more debt
This is the best day yet
Gonna travel 'round the world
My new story has unfurled

[Bridge]
Used to worry, used to stress
My whole life was just a mess
But now I'm flying high above
Filled with so much peace and love

[Record Scratch]

[Chorus]

[Hook]

[Chorus]

[Hook]

[Outro]

Homework & Practice

- **Task 1:** Listen carefully to your favorite songs and try to identify the specific catchy elements discussed in this chapter.

- **Task 2:** Generate all the variations of the "I Won the Lottery" case study in Suno. Compare how each step makes the song more catchy.

- **Task 3:** Choose a simple theme and use the principles from this chapter to create your own super-catchy song. Save it to your "My Songs" playlist.

- **Task 4:** Go to Suno's "Trending" section. Find 3 songs you think are very catchy and try to analyze *why* they are, based on the seven ingredients. Save them to your "Illustrative Songs" playlist.

- **Task 5:** Search for and listen to the song for this Chapter on the book's playlist: https://suno.com/playlist/0715eba6-45e6-4fe7-9893-4b38aa7780cc

Questions?

If you have questions about this chapter, ask the book's free companion chatbot. You can find the links in the Resources section of the book.

Chapter Summary

In this chapter, you learned the key ingredients that make a song catchy, from simplicity and repetition to the element of surprise. We explored how our brains are wired to love patterns and how you can use this to your advantage. You now have practical tips and templates to create infectious hooks and memorable melodies in Suno by using specific metatags and crafting targeted Style Prompts.

Now that you know how to make a song catchy, what if you want to make a song that sounds like one of your favorite hits? In the next chapter, we'll learn how to do just that by "Reverse Engineering Popular Songs."

Chapter 8: Reverse Engineering Popular Songs

In the last chapter, you learned the secrets to making catchy songs that get stuck in people's heads. But what if you want to create a song that has the *vibe* of one of your favorite hits? That's where a powerful learning technique called "reverse engineering" comes in. This chapter will teach you how to analyze the songs you love, extract their core ingredients, and use them as inspiration to create something brand new and totally you in Suno.

Chapter Outline

- Defining Reverse Engineering
- Ethical Considerations: Inspiration vs. Imitation
- Choosing a Famous Song
- Active Listening
- Extracting Key Lyrics Elements from a Song
- Extracting Key Music Elements from a Song
- Personalizing the New Song
- Case Study
- Homework

Defining Reverse Engineering

Ever wondered what makes your favorite song so good? Reverse engineering is like being a musical detective. It's the process of taking a song you admire, breaking it down into its essential parts, and understanding what makes it work. You'll look at its structure, its lyrical themes, and its musical style. Then, you'll use those insights not to copy the song, but to create a new one in Suno that captures a similar feeling, but with your own creative twist. It's one of the best ways to learn from the pros.

Ethical Considerations: Inspiration vs. Imitation

It is crucial to understand that reverse engineering is an educational tool, not a license to steal. The goal is to learn what makes a song great so you can apply those principles to your own original work.

Always remember the importance of originality. Directly copying someone else's lyrics or melodies is plagiarism, and it's not only unethical but can get you into legal trouble. We are not making cover songs here; we are creating new art.

The difference is simple: inspiration is taking the *feeling* of a song, while imitation is taking the *song*. For example, you might be inspired by the "sad, acoustic feel" of a ballad, but you wouldn't copy its exact chord progression and melody. You're borrowing the recipe, not stealing the cake.

Choosing a Famous Song

To use this method effectively, you need to pick a song that is famous enough for a chatbot to recognize. Chatbots are trained on vast amounts of public data, so they will know a lot about popular music but very little about obscure tracks.

Therefore, when choosing a song, consider these two elements:

- The song title must be well-known.
- The artist must also be famous.

Warning: If you choose a lesser-known song or artist, the chatbot will likely tell you it doesn't have enough information to provide an analysis.

Here are a few examples of songs that would work well for this process:

- "As It Was" by Harry Styles
- "Blinding Lights" by The Weeknd
- "Shape of You" by Ed Sheeran
- "Anti-Hero" by Taylor Swift
- "bad guy" by Billie Eilish
- "Don't Start Now" by Dua Lipa

Active Listening

Before you even touch a chatbot, you need to listen. Not just passively while you do other things, but *actively*. Once you've chosen your song, put on some headphones and give it your full attention.

Listen multiple times, focusing on different elements each time:

- **First Listen:** Focus on the overall vibe and emotion. How does it make you feel? Happy? Sad? Energetic?
- **Second Listen:** Focus on the lyrics. What is the story about? What are the key phrases that stand out?
- **Third Listen:** Focus on the beat and instruments. Is the tempo fast or slow? What instruments can you identify? What are the sonic textures like—is the sound clean, rough, warm, or cold?
- **Fourth Listen:** Focus on the structure. Can you identify the verses, the chorus, and a bridge? How is the song organized?

Take Notes: As you listen, write down your observations. Don't worry about using technical terms; just jot down what you notice. Your personal interpretation is a valuable part of this process.

Developing your own listening skills is crucial. Use the chatbot to automate the analysis, but always use your own ears and ideas to personalize the final result.

Extracting Key Lyrics Elements from a Song

Now, let's use an external chatbot (like ChatGPT, Claude, or Gemini) to get a detailed breakdown of the song's lyrics. The main elements of a lyrical analysis include the theme, mood, rhyme scheme, hooks, imagery, and structure.

Template prompt for lyrics analysis:

"Analyze the following elements from the song 'Song Name' by 'Artist' and extract the related information:

- *Genre*
- *Theme*
- *Mood*
- *Rhyme Scheme*
- *Hooks or Choruses*
- *Imagery & Figurative Language*
- *Structure including lines per section*

Show the analysis.

Lyrics Prompt Creation:
Based on your analysis, create a new lyrics prompt that can generate song lyrics in a style similar to the chosen song. Use the template below:

'Write a [genre] song about [theme] that incorporates [Mood], [Rhyme Scheme], [Lyrical Hooks], [Imagery & Figurative Language]. Use the [Structure] with a similar number of lines per section. Finally suggest a title for the song'

Show the generated lyrics prompt"

Note: Feel free to modify this template prompt to adapt it to your own artistic needs.

Warning: Chatbots may miscount the number of lines in a song. Always double-check each section manually, as errors can occur.

Example

Let's analyze the song "Birds of a Feather" by Billie Eilish. We'll use the first line of the template: "Analyze the following elements from the song 'Birds of a Feather' by 'Billie Eilish'..."

Here is a simulation of the chatbot's response:

Lyrics Analysis:

- **Genre:** Indie Pop, Alternative Pop
- **Theme:** Deep, unwavering love and companionship; sticking together through anything.
- **Mood:** Hopeful, affectionate, slightly dreamy, and optimistic.
- **Rhyme Scheme:** Primarily uses a mix of AABB and ABCB schemes, keeping it simple and memorable.

- **Hooks or Choruses:** The main hook is the phrase "Birds of a feather, we should stick together," which is repeated for emphasis.

- **Imagery & Figurative Language:** Uses imagery of "weather" to represent life's challenges and the "birds of a feather" metaphor for inseparable companionship.

- **Structure:** Intro, Verse 1 (4 lines), Chorus (4 lines), Verse 2 (4 lines), Chorus (4 lines), Bridge (4 lines), Chorus (4 lines), Outro.

New Lyrics Prompt:

Write an Indie Pop song about lifelong friendship that incorporates a hopeful and affectionate mood, a simple AABB rhyme scheme, a repetitive lyrical hook about being inseparable, and imagery of journeys and changing seasons. Use the structure: Intro (4 lines), Verse 1 (4 lines), Chorus (4 lines), Verse 2 (4 lines), Chorus (4 lines), Bridge (4 lines), Chorus (4 lines), Outro (4 lines). Finally suggest a title for the song.

Once you have this prompt, you can use it in any chatbot to generate a new set of lyrics inspired by the original song.

Extracting Key Music Elements from a Song

Next, we'll use a chatbot to analyze the *music* itself. This includes the genre, tempo, instruments, and production techniques.

Template prompt for music analysis:

"Analyze the following elements from the song 'Song Name' by 'Artist':

- *Musical Style: Provide a brief analysis covering: Genre/Subgenre, Tempo, Mood, Instruments, Sonic Textures, Vocals, and Production Techniques.*

- *Present your findings clearly.*

- *Based on your analysis, create a new style prompt that generates song lyrics similar in style to the chosen song. Use the template below and ensure the prompt to generate the style prompt.*

'(Decade/Era) [Genre/Subgenre] with a [Tempo], [Mood] feel, featuring [Instruments], [Sonic Textures], [Vocals] and [Production Techniques]'"

Note: Feel free to modify this template prompt to adapt it to your own artistic needs.

Example

Let's analyze "Birds of a Feather" by Billie Eilish again, this time for its music. We'll use the first line of the template: "Analyze the following elements from the song 'Birds of a Feather' by 'Billie Eilish'..."

Here is a simulation of the chatbot's response:

Music Analysis:

- **Genre/Subgenre:** Indie Pop, Synth-Pop.

- **Tempo:** Upbeat, around 120-125 BPM.

- **Mood:** Joyful, optimistic, lighthearted.

- **Instruments:** Prominent synth bassline, steady electronic drum beat, shimmering synth pads, and subtle keyboard melodies.

- **Sonic Textures:** Clean, crisp, and polished with a warm and bright feel.

- **Vocals:** Billie Eilish's signature soft, breathy lead vocal with layered harmonies in the chorus.
- **Production Techniques:** Modern, polished production with a wide stereo image and clear separation between elements.

New Style Prompt:

2020s Indie Pop with an Upbeat Tempo, a Joyful and Optimistic feel, featuring a [prominent synth bassline], [steady electronic drum beat], and [shimmering synth pads], a Clean and Bright sonic texture, soft, breathy female vocals with [layered harmonies], and a Polished, Modern Production.

Personalizing the New Song

Now you have a new set of lyrics and a new style prompt. This is where your creativity comes in. Using the notes you took during your active listening, you can personalize these AI-generated prompts.

Lyrics Personalization

Review the lyrics generated by the chatbot. Do they fit your vision? You can change words, rewrite lines, or add new metatags to better match your ideas. Maybe you noticed a cool rhythmic pause in the original song that the chatbot missed; now's your chance to add it in with a line break! Generate the lyrics iteratively until you are satisfied with the result.

Music Personalization

Review the style prompt. Does it capture the feeling you want? Maybe you heard a subtle acoustic guitar in the original song that you want to include. You can add [Acoustic Guitar] to the prompt. Perhaps you want the song to feel a bit more "raw" instead of "polished." Change the keyword! Once you have refined the lyrics and the style prompt, generate the song in Suno. Compare it to the original and refine it again if you want.

Case Study

Let's reverse engineer the song **"Espresso" by Sabrina Carpenter.**

Extract Lyrics Elements

- **Lyrics Analysis:**
    - **Genre:** Disco-Pop, Funk-Pop.
    - **Theme:** Having an irresistible and captivating effect on someone; confidence and self-assurance.
    - **Mood:** Playful, confident, flirty, and energetic.
    - **Rhyme Scheme:** Mostly AABB in the verses, very simple and direct.
    - **Hooks or Choruses:** The main hook is the memorable line, "That's that me, espresso."
    - **Imagery & Figurative Language:** Uses coffee metaphors ("espresso," "mocha," "latte") to describe her effect on a lover.
    - **Structure:** Intro, Verse 1, Pre-Chorus, Chorus, Verse 2, Pre-Chorus, Chorus, Bridge, Chorus, Outro.
- **Generated Lyrics Prompt:**

Write a Disco-Pop song about feeling confident and magnetic. Incorporate a playful and flirty mood, a simple AABB rhyme scheme, a repetitive hook about being unforgettable, and clever metaphors related to desserts or candy. Use the structure: Intro, Verse, Pre-Chorus, Chorus, Verse, Pre-Chorus, Chorus, Bridge, Chorus, Outro. Use 4 lines per section. Suggest a title for the song.

Extract Music Elements

- **Music Analysis:**

    o **Genre/Subgenre:** Disco-Pop, Nu-Disco.

    o **Tempo:** Groovy, mid-tempo, around 115-120 BPM.

    o **Mood:** Fun, summery, confident, and carefree.

    o **Instruments:** A very prominent and groovy bassline, a simple four-on-the-floor drum beat, funky electric guitar riffs, and shimmering synths.

    o **Sonic Textures:** Warm, polished, and crisp.

    o **Vocals:** Light, slightly breathy female lead vocal with layered, chorus-effect harmonies.

    o **Production Techniques:** Modern production with a retro 70s disco feel; clean and punchy mix.

- **Generated Style Prompt:**

    70s Nu-Disco with a Groovy Mid-Tempo, a Fun and Confident feel, featuring a [prominent groovy bassline], [funky electric guitar riffs], and [shimmering synths], a Warm and Polished sonic texture, light, breathy female vocals with [layered harmonies], and a Modern Production with a retro feel.

Personalize the Generated Lyrics Prompt

- **Personalized Lyrics Prompt:**
  Write a Nu-Disco song about being the life of the party. Incorporate a fun and energetic mood, a simple AABB rhyme scheme, a repetitive hook about lighting up the room, and clever metaphors related to electricity or fireworks. Use the structure: Intro, Verse, Pre-Chorus, Chorus, Verse, Pre-Chorus, Chorus, Bridge, Chorus, Outro. . Use 4 short lines per section. Suggest the title "Electric Love."

Personalize the Generated Style Prompt

- **Personalized Style Prompt:**
  70s Nu-Disco with a Groovy, Upbeat Tempo, a Fun and Energetic feel, featuring a [SUPER funky slap bassline], [clean electric guitar licks], and [bright piano chords], a Crisp and Polished sonic texture, breathy female lead vocals with [disco diva harmonies], and a Modern, Punchy Production.

Final Lyrics Generated from Personalized Prompt:

/* Song Title: "Electric Love" */

[Intro]
(Yeah, feel the charge)
(Ooh)

[Verse]
Walk into the room, yeah
Flipping on a switch
Everyone can feel it
That little magic twitch

[Pre-Chorus]
The air begins to crackle
A current you can feel

My energy is rising
You know this feeling's real

[Chorus]
They call me electric love
A fire in the dark
A human firework
Leaving my own spark

[Verse]
The dance floor starts to rumble
The beat is taking hold
A story to be written
In flashes, bright and bold

[Pre-Chorus]
The energy is building
A current you can't fight
I'm glowing in the darkness
A bolt of neon light

[Chorus]
They call me electric love
A fire in the dark
A human firework
Leaving my own spark

[Bridge]
No need for any wires
No need for any plug
My power's from within me
A human lightning bug

[Chorus]
They call me electric love
A fire in the dark
A human firework
Leaving my own spark

[Outro]

Now, you can take these new lyrics and the personalized style prompt, generate the song in Suno, and compare it to the original "Espresso" to see how you've captured a similar vibe while creating something new.

Homework

- **Task 1:** Generate the song from the "Espresso" case study in Suno using the final personalized lyrics and style prompt. Compare it to the original song. How close did you get to the vibe?

- **Task 2:** Choose a popular song you love and use the reverse engineering method to create your own inspired track. Make the song public on Suno and ask your friends for feedback!

- **Task 3:** Search for and listen to the song for this Chapter on the book's playlist: https://suno.com/playlist/0715eba6-45e6-4fe7-9893-4b38aa7780cc

Questions?

If you have questions about this chapter, ask the book's free companion chatbot. You can find the links in the Resources section of the book.

Chapter Summary

In this chapter, you learned the powerful technique of reverse engineering. You saw how to actively listen to a song, use a chatbot to analyze its lyrical and musical elements, and then use those insights to create a brand-new song in Suno. Most importantly, you learned how to use this process for inspiration while still creating something original and personal.

You now have all the core skills to create amazing music with Suno. In the final chapter, we'll look at how you can take these skills and potentially turn your musical creations into a source of income. Get ready to learn about "From Beats to Bucks - Make Money with Suno."

Chapter 9: From Beats to Bucks - Make Money with Suno

In the last chapter, you learned how to reverse engineer your favorite songs to understand what makes them hits. You now have a complete set of skills to create almost any kind of music you can imagine. But what if making music could be more than just a hobby? This chapter is about turning your new passion into a potential paycheck.

Chapter Outline

- Suno can be More Than Just a Hobby
- Ways to Create Value with Custom Music
- Transitioning from Value to Income
- Monetization Strategies
- Building Your Suno Brand
- Important Considerations for the Suno Entrepreneur
- Case Study: From Birthday Gift to First Gig
- Homework

Suno can be More Than Just a Hobby

You've learned to create catchy songs, heartfelt ballads, and everything in between. This is more than just a cool party trick—it's a superpower. You now have the ability to create custom music on demand, which can be your new side hustle or, who knows, maybe even your main hustle.

To understand how, let's talk about value versus price. **Value** is subjective; it's the personal importance or worth of something to an individual. **Price** is objective; it's the amount of money asked for in exchange for something. Music creates priceless emotional value. When you make a song for your family, you're delivering that value for free. But others, who don't have your skills, are often willing to pay a price for that same value.

What Makes Music Valuable?

Music evokes emotion, creates memories, and connects people. A song can make you feel happy on a bad day, remind you of a special moment, or become the anthem for your group of friends. This emotional connection is its inherent value. The "price" is simply what someone is willing to offer for that feeling, but the true value can be far greater.

Ways to Create Value with Custom Music

Create Value for Yourself
First and foremost, you can create value for yourself. Is there a particular song you wish existed but no one has made yet? Make it! Now you can build a personal music library perfectly tailored to your own tastes.

Create Value to your Family
You can create priceless memories for your family members. A custom song is a unique and deeply personal gift. The "goosebumps" factor—the emotional impact of a song made just for them—is incredibly powerful.

- Create unique birthday songs for your partner, children, parents or relatives.

- Compose a one-of-a-kind anniversary song for your partner.

- Make a special graduation song to celebrate your kids' achievements.

Create value For Friends & Fun
Strengthen your connections with friends through personalized music.

- Become the life of the party by making custom tracks for friends' celebrations.

- Create inside-joke anthems that only your inner circle will understand.

- Reconnect with old friends you haven't seen in a while with a song that recalls your shared memories.

Create value For Co-workers & Bosses
You can even strengthen bonds at work with custom music. Compose a fun birthday song for a co-worker to share a laugh. And just imagine your boss's reaction if you created a personalized birthday song for her or him—who knows, it might just get you that raise or promotion!

Music is the New Valuable Currency

Custom music delivers memorable experiences and strengthens bonds. This "emotional currency" is incredibly valuable, even when no money changes hands.

Transitioning from Value to Income

If your custom songs bring joy to your family and friends, that's a great sign that others might pay for a similar service. This is how you transition from creating personal value to creating market value.

Commercial License Requirement

This is the most important rule: to sell *anything* made with Suno, you **MUST** have a subscription (Pro or Premier) that grants you commercial rights. Using creations made with the free version of Suno for profit is against their terms of service. Always check the latest licensing rules on their website to be sure.

Monetization Strategies

Here are four main ways you can start making money with your Suno creations.

1. Selling Your Original Music Directly

- **Platforms like Bandcamp:** Bandcamp is a fantastic platform for independent artists. It allows you to sell digital downloads and even physical merchandise. With Suno, you can create full albums, EPs, or singles and sell them directly to fans.

- **Your Own Website / Online Store:** Platforms like Shopify or Gumroad make it easy to set up a simple online store. You can even use simple PayPal buttons on a personal website to sell your tracks directly.

- **Streaming Services (Spotify, Apple Music, etc.):** With a commercial license, you can use a music distributor like DistroKid or TuneCore to get your Suno-created music onto all the major streaming platforms.

    - **Warning:** The world of AI-generated music is new and policies are still being formed. Before you sign up with a music distributor, contact their customer support and ask if they allow the distribution of AI-generated music. This can save you from potential issues down the road.

    - **Tip:** If you want to be extra safe and have some money to invest, you can download your song (or even better, its individual stems) and hire a musician on a freelance site like Fiverr to recreate it without AI. If you purchase all the rights to this new human-made version, you can submit it to streaming services with confidence.

2. Offering Creative Services (Freelancing)

- **Freelance Platforms (Fiverr, Upwork, etc.):** You can list your services as a "Custom Songwriter" or "AI Music Composer."
    - **Music for Individuals:** Offer packages for custom birthday songs, wedding songs, anniversary gifts, or graduation anthems.
    - **Music for Businesses & Creators:** Create jingles and intro/outro music for local businesses, podcasts, and YouTube channels. Provide background music for vloggers, streamers, or indie game developers. Make short, catchy tracks for TikToks, Instagram Reels, and social media ads.

3. Content Creation & Community Building (Indirect Monetization)

- **YouTube/TikTok/Instagram Creator:** Create a channel focused on a specific niche (like funny pet videos, gaming highlights, or chill study music) and use your original Suno music as the soundtrack.
    - **Monetization Methods:** As your channel grows, you can earn money from ad revenue, brand sponsorships, or by using a platform like Patreon to offer exclusive content to your biggest fans.

4. Licensing Your Music for Media

- This is a more advanced topic, but you can submit your original tracks to royalty-free music libraries like Pond5 or AudioJungle. When someone licenses your track for their project, you get paid. This can be a competitive field, but it has the potential for long-term passive income.

Building Your Suno Brand

Find Your Niche
What are you passionate about? Do you love making humorous songs, emotional ballads, or music for a specific genre like lofi or synthwave? Finding a niche can help you stand out.

Quality Control
AI can generate music quickly, but always offer your best work. For any commercial purpose, be sure to download the WAV version of your song, as it has better audio quality than an MP3. Use Suno's editing features to polish your tracks before you release them.

Create a Portfolio
Use Suno playlists, a Bandcamp page, or a simple website to showcase your best creations. This will be your resume when offering your services.

Basic Self-Promotion
Start with the people you know. Share the custom songs you make for family and friends. This can lead to great word-of-mouth promotion. Share snippets of your work on social media and engage with online music communities.

Important Considerations for the Suno Entrepreneur

- **Understanding Copyright:** With a commercial license, you own the copyright to the unique songs you create (the combination of your original lyrics and Suno's output). However, Suno owns its AI model. Always follow their official terms of service.

- **Be Original:** The more unique your prompts and lyrics are, the more original your final song will be. This reduces the chance of creating something that sounds too similar to another track.

- **Patience and Persistence:** Building an income stream from music takes time and consistent effort. Don't get discouraged if you don't become a star overnight.
- **Stay Updated:** Suno is constantly evolving. Keep an eye on their official blog (https://suno.com/blog) for announcements about new features and any changes to their terms.

Case Study: From Birthday Gift to First Gig

Here are a few examples of the kinds of custom songs you can create for different occasions.

Birthday Song Example

[Verse]
Another year has come and gone
A new day dawns, a brand new song
We're here to celebrate with you
And make your special wish come true

[Chorus]
Happy birthday, happy birthday
May your heart be light and free
Happy birthday, happy birthday
From all of us, from you to me

[Verse]
Blow the candles, make a wish
Seal it with a happy kiss
May your year be filled with cheer
The best one yet, have no fear

- **Style Prompt:** Upbeat Pop, joyful mood, simple and catchy melody, with acoustic guitar and hand claps

Wedding Song Example

[Verse]
Two hearts together, beating now as one
A new life started, beneath the morning sun
A promise spoken, a gentle, loving vow
Forever starts right here, forever starts right now

[Chorus]
This is your love story
Written in the stars
A perfect masterpiece
No matter where you are

[Verse]
Through every season, through every single day
May your love keep growing, in every single way
Hand in hand together, walking through the years
Sharing all the laughter, wiping all the tears

- **Style Prompt:** Romantic Pop Ballad, slow tempo, emotional female vocal, featuring piano and soaring strings

Jingle Song Example

[Verse]
Looking for a brand new ride?
Don't know where to turn?
Feeling lost and confused?
Got a lesson left to learn?

[Chorus]
Come on down to Honest Bob's!
The best deals in the town!
Come on down to Honest Bob's!
He will never let you down!

[Verse]
He's got trucks and he's got cars
Vans and SUVs

The best prices in the state
He'll give you brand new keys!

- **Style Prompt:** Catchy 80s Rock jingle, upbeat and energetic, powerful male vocal, with electric guitars and a driving drum beat

Homework

- **Task 1:** Run the songs from the Case Study in Suno. Notice how the style prompt changes the feel for each occasion.

- **Task 2:** Create a commemorative song for a loved one (it could be for a birthday, anniversary, or just because!). Put your heart into it and save it in your "My Songs" playlist.

- **Task 3:** Explore a freelance site like Fiverr or Upwork. Search for "custom song" or "AI music" to see what services other people are offering and at what prices. Take notes for your own potential offerings.

- **Task 4:** Contact the customer support for a music distributor like CDBaby, TuneCore, or DistroKid and ask them directly if they currently support the distribution of AI-generated music.

- **Task 5:** Listen to the chapter's song on the book's playlist: https://suno.com/playlist/0715eba6-45e6-4fe7-9893-4b38aa7780cc

Questions?

If you have questions about this chapter, ask the book's free companion chatbot (you can find the links in the Resources section).

Chapter Summary

Congratulations! You've reached the end of your introductory journey. In this chapter, you learned that your new music-making skills have real-world value. We explored different ways you can monetize your Suno creations, from selling your music directly to offering freelance services. We also covered the importance of having a commercial license, finding your niche, and building a brand.

You now have all the foundational knowledge you need to create amazing, catchy, and inspired music with Suno AI, and you even have a roadmap for how you might turn that passion into profit. The world of AI music is just beginning, and you are now officially a part of it. Keep creating, keep experimenting, and most importantly, have fun

Appendices

Chatbots of the Book

Congratulations on completing your journey from listener to composer!

You now have a powerful new creative skill, and I sincerely hope this guide made the process fun and rewarding.

If you found this book valuable, I would be incredibly grateful if you took a moment to leave a review on the book's website. Your feedback and insights aren't just helpful for me—they're a beacon for other beginners who are just starting out, showing them what's possible.

Thank you for letting me be a part of your musical beginning. Now go on and start surprising people with your new skills!

The book has 3 chatbot in different models so you can use the one you feel comfortable:

- GPT-4o-mini;

    https://poe.com/Suno_4_Everyone_4oEn

- Claude-Haiku:

    https://poe.com/Suno_4_Everyone_HEn

- Gemini-Flash:

    https://poe.com/Suno_4_Everyone_GEn

Appendix A: Genres & Subgenres

This list showcases a wide range of genres and styles that Suno can create. Experiment and find your favorites! Remember, you can combine styles and use descriptive language to create unique sounds.

Genre	Style/Subgenre
Acoustic	Acoustic Pop, Acoustic Rock, Singer-Songwriter, Folk
Alternative	Alternative Rock, Indie Rock, Grunge, Emo
Ambient	Ambient, Chillwave, Soundscape, Atmospheric
Blues	Blues, Electric Blues, Blues Rock, Delta Blues
Children's Music	Children's Songs, Lullabies, Nursery Rhymes
Classical	Classical, Orchestral, Symphony, Chamber Music
Country	Country, Country Pop, Country Rock, Bluegrass, Honky Tonk
Dance	Dance, Electronic Dance Music (EDM), House, Techno, Trance
Electronic	Electronica, Synthwave, Trip Hop
Folk	Folk, Folk Rock, Indie Folk, Celtic Music
Funk	Funk, Soul Funk, Disco Funk
Gospel	Gospel, Contemporary Gospel, Southern Gospel
Hip Hop	Hip Hop, Rap, Trap, Lo-Fi Hip Hop, Gangsta Rap
Indie	Indie Pop, Indie Rock, Dream Pop
Jazz	Jazz, Swing, Smooth Jazz, Latin Jazz
Latin	Salsa, Merengue, Bachata, Reggaeton, Cumbia, Tango
Metal	Heavy Metal, Death Metal, Black Metal, Progressive Metal
Opera	Opera, Classical Opera, Romantic Opera
Pop	Pop, Synth Pop, Pop Rock, Indie Pop, K-Pop, J-Pop
R&B/Soul	R&B, Soul, Motown, Neo Soul
Reggae	Reggae, Dub, Roots Reggae, Dancehall
Rock	Rock, Classic Rock, Hard Rock, Punk Rock
World	World Music, Afrobeat, Flamenco, Celtic, Indian Classical

Annex B: Main Suno's Metatags

This guide provides an overview of the main metatags you can use in Suno to direct your song's composition. Remember, Suno's AI interprets these tags within the overall context of your song, so results can vary. Experimentation is key!

Song Structure Tags

Metatag	Description
[Break]	A short pause or change in the music, often just for a few beats.
[Bridge]	A section that connects parts of the song, often with a different feel.
[Chorus]	The main, repeatable section of the song that contains the central message.
[End]	Instructs the AI to create a clear, abrupt ending to the song.
[Fade Out]	Tells the AI to gradually decrease the volume to a gentle close.
[Hook]	Highlights a short, catchy phrase or melody you want to be memorable.
[Instrumental]	Creates a section with only instruments and no singing.
[Interlude]	A longer instrumental section that can create a shift in mood.
[Intro]	The beginning section that sets the stage and mood for the song.
[Outro]	The concluding section that brings the song to a satisfying finish.
[Pre-Chorus]	A short section that builds anticipation leading into the chorus.
[Refrain]	A repeated line or phrase, often used at the end of a verse.
[Verse]	The sections of the song that tell the story and develop the narrative.

Instrumental Tags

Metatag	Description
[Acoustic Guitar]	Specifies the use of an acoustic guitar.
[Bass]	Specifies the use of a bass guitar.
[Drums]	Specifies the use of drums.
[Electric Guitar]	Specifies the use of an electric guitar.
[Horns]	Specifies brass instruments like trumpets or trombones.
[Organ]	Specifies the use of an organ (e.g., Hammond B3).
[Percussion Break]	Creates a section focused on a drum or percussion solo.
[Piano]	Specifies the use of a piano.
[Strings]	Specifies string instruments like violins or cellos.
[Synth]	Specifies the use of a synthesizer.

Vocal Tags

Metatag	Description
[Ad-libs]	Adds spontaneous-sounding vocal interjections (e.g., "oh yeah").
[Choir]	Instructs a group of voices to sing together.
[Female Vocals]	Specifies that a female voice should sing a particular part.
[Harmonies]	Adds background vocals that support the main melody.
[Male Vocals]	Specifies that a male voice should sing a particular part.
[Narration]	A spoken-word style used for storytelling.
[Rapped Verse]	Delivers the lyrics in a rap style.
[Spoken Word]	General tag for spoken, non-sung lyrics.
[Sultry Vocals]	Creates a smooth, seductive, often breathy vocal style.
[Whispered]	Makes the vocal delivery a soft, intimate whisper.

Tempo & Dynamics Tags

Metatag	Description
[Build]	Gradually increases the energy and intensity of the music.
[Crescendo]	Gradually increases the volume of the music.
[Decrescendo]	Gradually decreases the volume of the music.
[Drop]	A common EDM feature where the bass and drums suddenly kick in.
[Faster]	Increases the tempo (speed) of the music.
[Louder]	Increases the volume or intensity of a section.
[Slower]	Decreases the tempo (speed) of the music.
[Softer]	Decreases the volume or intensity of a section.

Special Effects Tags

Metatag	Description
[Autotune]	Applies the iconic pitch-correction effect to vocals.
[Delay]	Creates repeating, rhythmic echoes on a voice or instrument.
[Distortion]	Adds a gritty, fuzzy, or overdriven sound, common in rock.
[Echo]	Adds a distinct, repeating echo effect.
[Reverb]	Adds a sense of space or echo, like singing in a large hall.
[Telephone Effect]	Makes the vocal sound like it's coming through a telephone.
[Vocaloid]	Creates a robotic or synthesized voice sound.
[Vocoder]	Creates a classic robotic vocal effect by blending a voice with a synth.

Appendix C: Moods for Style Prompts

This list provides a spectrum of common moods you can use in your Style Prompts to guide the emotional feel of your music.

Mood	Description
Joyful	Full of happiness and celebration. Creates very bright, cheerful music.
Upbeat	Positive and energetic, with a rhythm that makes you want to tap your feet.
Energetic	High-octane and powerful. Think of workout music or an action movie scene.
Playful	Lighthearted, fun, and often whimsical or bouncy.
Uplifting	Creates a feeling of hope and positivity, making you feel inspired.
Hopeful	Suggests optimism and looking forward to something good.
Romantic	Evokes feelings of love, affection, and tenderness.
Relaxed	A calm, easy-going vibe. Perfect for music to unwind to.
Calm	Creates a sense of peace, quiet, and tranquility.
Mellow	Smooth, soft, and gentle, without any harsh sounds.
Epic	Creates a grand, cinematic feel, like a soundtrack for a huge adventure.
Dramatic	Full of tension, emotion, and excitement.
Suspenseful	Builds tension and makes the listener feel like something is about to happen.
Mysterious	Creates a sense of wonder, intrigue, or the unknown.
Haunting	Eerie and memorable, often with a beautiful but slightly sad or ghostly feel.
Melancholy	A gentle, thoughtful sadness. More reflective than purely sad.
Sad	Directly evokes feelings of sorrow, loss, or heartbreak.
Somber	Very serious, solemn, and often dark in tone.
Dark	Creates a gloomy, heavy, or even sinister atmosphere.

Annex D: Tempo Keywords

This table groups different tempo terms—from traditional Italian to modern and expressive—by their approximate Beats Per Minute (BPM). Use these keywords in your Style Prompt to guide the speed and feel of your music.

Italian Term	Modern Term	Expressive Term	BPM Range
Grave			20–40 BPM
Largo	Very Slow		40–60 BPM
Adagio	Slow	Mellow, Chill, Laid-back, Laid Back, Dark	60–90 BPM
Andante, Moderato	Moderate, Medium	Mellow, Laid-back, Laid Back, Groovy, Hype, Uplifting, Dark	90–120 BPM
Allegro	Fast	Upbeat, Groovy, Driving, Hype, Uplifting, Club Energy	120–140 BPM
Allegro, Vivace	Very Fast	Driving, Aggressive, High Energy, Club Energy	140–168 BPM
Vivace, Presto		Aggressive, High Energy	168–200+ BPM

Annex E: Vocal Keywords

This guide covers the main keywords you can use in your Style Prompt to describe the voice you want in your song. These terms help you control everything from vocal texture to emotional delivery and character roles.

Gender & Age

Keyword	Description
Child Vocals	A voice resembling that of a young child (can be difficult to generate consistently).
Female Vocals	A singing voice with female characteristics.
Male Vocals	A singing voice with male characteristics.

Vocal Quality & Texture

Keyword	Description
Airy	A light, breathy, and soft vocal quality.
Breathy	A soft vocal style where the sound of the singer's breath is audible.
Clear	A pure, crisp, and easy-to-understand vocal, free of roughness.
Deep	A low-pitched, resonant voice with a full-bodied sound.
Ethereal	A delicate, heavenly, and almost otherworldly vocal sound.
Gritty	A rough, textured voice with a bit of "gravel" or raspiness.
High-Pitched	A voice that sits in a high register or range.
Raspy	A rough, hoarse-sounding vocal quality.
Smooth	A fluid, polished, and seamless vocal delivery, free of harshness.

Singing Style & Delivery

Keyword	Description
Belting	A powerful, loud, and sustained singing style, often used for big choruses.
Chanting	Rhythmic, repetitive speaking or singing, often by a group.
Falsetto	A male singing technique used to sing notes in a very high, airy range.
Narration	Spoken-word delivery, as if telling a story.
Operatic	A powerful, formal, and dramatic vocal style used in opera.
Rapping	Rhythmic, rhyming speech delivered over a beat.
Screaming	An aggressive, shouted vocal style, common in rock, punk, and metal.
Spoken Word	Lyrics that are spoken rather than sung.
Whispering	A very soft, quiet, and intimate vocal delivery.

Emotional Tone

Keyword	Description
Aggressive	A forceful, intense, and often confrontational vocal delivery.
Emotional	A delivery full of feeling and expression, clearly showing an emotional state.
Passionate	An intense and heartfelt vocal delivery that shows strong feelings.
Soulful	Expresses deep, authentic emotion, common in soul, blues, and R&B genres.
Sultry	A smooth, seductive, and alluring vocal style.

Personas & Characters

Keyword	Description
Announcer	A clear, formal voice, like a radio host or event announcer.
Choir	A group of singers performing together in harmony.
Diva	A powerful, dramatic, and commanding female vocal performance.

Drill Sergeant	A harsh, barking, and authoritative voice.
Lounge Singer	A smooth, crooning style reminiscent of a classic jazz club singer.
Narrator	A voice that tells a story in a spoken-word style.
Storyteller	A conversational and engaging voice that focuses on telling a tale.
Villain	A menacing, dark, or evil-sounding character voice.

Vocal Effects

Keyword	Description
Autotune	Applies a robotic, pitch-corrected vocal effect.
Reverb	Adds echo and a sense of space, like singing in a large hall or cave.
Vocaloid	Creates a distinctly synthesized, robotic anime-style singing voice.
Vocoder	A classic robotic vocal effect created by blending a voice with a synthesizer.

Appendix F: Instrument Keywords

This appendix lists common instrument keywords you can use in your Style Prompts to tell Suno what kind of sound you want. Don't be afraid to combine them to create your perfect band!

String Instruments (Guitars & Bass)

Keyword	Description
Acoustic Guitar	The standard, classic sound of a non-electric guitar.
Bass Guitar	The low-pitched instrument that provides the foundation of the rhythm.
Clean Guitar	An electric guitar sound without any fuzzy distortion; bright and clear.

Distorted Guitar	An electric guitar with a fuzzy, heavy sound, perfect for rock and metal.
Electric Guitar	The standard sound of an electric guitar, used in most popular music.
Slide Guitar	A guitar played with a metal or glass slide for a smooth, "sliding" sound.
Upright Bass	The large, acoustic bass used in jazz, classical, and early rockabilly.

String Instruments (Orchestral & Folk)

Keyword	Description
Banjo	A stringed instrument with a bright, twangy sound common in country and folk.
Cello	A large string instrument with a deep, rich, and warm tone.
Fiddle	Another name for a violin, especially when played in a country or folk style.
Harp	A large instrument with many strings, known for its angelic, plucked sound.
Strings	A general term for the orchestral string section (violins, violas, cellos).
Ukulele	A small, four-stringed guitar with a light, happy sound.
Violin	The classic high-pitched orchestral string instrument.

Keyboard Instruments

Keyword	Description
Accordion	A portable instrument with a keyboard and bellows, used in folk and polka.
Electric Piano	The sound of a digital piano, often with a smoother, bell-like quality.
Organ	A keyboard with a rich, sustained sound, from church organs to rock organs.
Piano	The classic acoustic piano sound, versatile for any genre.

Percussion Instruments

Keyword	Description
808 Bass	The deep, booming bass drum from the TR-808, essential in hip-hop and trap.
Bongos / Congas	Hand drums that create the signature rhythmic feel of Latin music.
Drum Machine	The sound of a classic electronic drum kit.
Drums / Drum Kit	The standard set of drums and cymbals used in most genres.
Electronic Drums	The crisp, modern sound of a digital drum kit.
Hand Claps	The sound of clapping hands, used as a rhythmic element instead of a snare.
Tambourine	A small frame with metal jingles, adds a high-end shimmer to the rhythm.

Wind Instruments

Keyword	Description
Clarinet	A single-reed woodwind instrument common in jazz and classical music.
Flute	A high-pitched woodwind with a clear, airy sound.
Harmonica	A small mouth organ often used in blues, folk, and country.
Horns	A general term for a section of brass instruments like trumpets and trombones.
Saxophone / Sax	A versatile instrument known for its smooth sound, essential in jazz and pop.
Trombone	A lower-pitched brass instrument with a distinct slide.
Trumpet	A high-pitched brass instrument with a bright, piercing sound.

Electronic Instruments & Effects

Keyword	Description
Record Scratch	The "wicky-wicky" sound of a DJ scratching vinyl, a staple in hip-hop.

Synth	Short for synthesizer, an electronic instrument that can create a huge variety of sounds.
Synth Bass	A bass line played on a synthesizer instead of a bass guitar.
Synth Lead	The main melody or hook of a song, played on a synthesizer.
Synth Pad	A sustained, atmospheric synthesizer sound that creates a background texture.

Appendix G: Sonic Textures

Use these keywords in your Style Prompts to describe the overall quality, feel, and character of the sound. Combining these with genre, mood, and instruments will give you incredible control over the final track.

Sound Quality & Fidelity

These keywords describe the clarity and production style of the music.

Keyword	Description
Clean	A polished and clear sound, without added fuzz or effects.
Distorted	A fuzzy, gritty, or overdriven sound, common in rock and electronic music.
Gritty	A rough, slightly raw sound texture, adding a bit of an edge.
Hi-Fi	"High-Fidelity." A very clean, professional, and high-quality studio sound.
Lo-Fi	"Low-Fidelity." Intentionally imperfect, often with a warm, vintage, or slightly muffled quality.
Raw	An unpolished, direct, and unprocessed sound, as if recorded live.

Density & Space

These keywords relate to how full or empty the arrangement sounds.

Keyword	Description
Dense	A very full sound with many instruments and layers packed closely together.
Layered	Features multiple overlapping parts or instruments that build on each other.
Lush	A rich, full, and often beautiful sound with many layers of instruments or harmonies.
Minimal / Minimalist	Uses very few sounds or instruments, creating a simple and uncluttered feel.
Spacious	Creates a feeling of openness and space, often with the use of reverb and echo.
Sparse	The opposite of lush; uses few instruments, creating a feeling of emptiness.

Atmospheric & Environmental

These keywords create a strong sense of place, feeling, or environment.

Keyword	Description
Ambient	Focuses on tone and atmosphere over traditional structure; often used for background music.
Atmospheric	Creates a distinct mood or feeling of being in a specific environment.
Cinematic	A grand, sweeping sound that feels like it belongs in a movie soundtrack.
Dreamy	Creates a soft, hazy, and often surreal or fantasy-like quality.
Ethereal	A very light, delicate, and "heavenly" sound, seeming to come from another world.
Haunting	A beautiful but slightly eerie or melancholic sound that stays with you.

Tonal Color & Temperature

These keywords describe the overall "color" or character of the sound.

Keyword Description

Bright	A sound with more high-end frequencies; sounds crisp, clear, and sharp.
Cold	A sound that can feel distant, electronic, or stark, with less warmth or bass.
Dark	A sound with more low-end frequencies; can feel gloomy, serious, or mysterious.
Warm	A pleasant, rich sound with more bass and mid-range frequencies, like a vinyl record.

Rhythmic Feel & Movement

These keywords describe the texture and momentum of the rhythm.

Keyword	Description
Driving	A strong, persistent rhythm that relentlessly pushes the song forward.
Glitchy	Incorporates digital errors like stutters and skips as a rhythmic element.
Hypnotic	A repetitive, mesmerizing rhythm that draws the listener in.
Pulsing	A rhythm that feels like a steady, throbbing pulse or heartbeat.
Syncopated	A rhythm that emphasizes the off-beats, creating a funky or groovy feel.

Appendix H: Production Techniques

These keywords describe the studio methods and effects used to shape the final sound of a track. Use them in your Style Prompts to add a professional polish or a creative twist to your music.

Spatial & Time-Based Effects

These techniques manipulate the sense of space, depth, and repetition in your music.

Keyword	Description
Echo	Creates distinct, repeating copies of a sound, like shouting in a canyon.
Delay	Creates rhythmic, repeating echoes. Can be used to create complex patterns.
Reverb	Adds a sense of space and ambiance, like the sound is in a specific room (hall, cathedral, small room).
Slapback Delay	A very short, single echo that "slaps back" immediately. Common in vintage rock 'n' roll.

Modulation & Texture Effects

These effects add movement, character, and texture to a sound.

Keyword	Description
Chorus Effect	Makes a sound thicker and shimmer, as if multiple voices or instruments are playing at once.
Flanger	Creates a sweeping, "jet plane" or "whooshing" sound effect.
Phaser	Creates a swirling, watery sound that sweeps through the frequencies.
Tremolo	A rapid, "trembling" effect created by turning the volume up and down quickly.

Vibrato	A slight and rapid wavering in pitch, adding expression to vocals or instruments.
Wah / Wah Pedal	The classic guitar effect that sounds like the instrument is saying "wah-wah."

Dynamic & Tonal Shaping

These keywords control the volume balance and frequency content of the track.

Keyword	Description
Boomy Bass	Emphasizes the very low frequencies for a deep, resonant bass sound.
Compression	Evens out the volume, making quiet parts louder and loud parts quieter for a punchy, polished sound.
Crisp Highs	Emphasizes the high frequencies, making the track sound brighter and clearer.
Saturation	Adds warmth and subtle distortion, mimicking the pleasing sound of vintage analog equipment.
Scooped Mids	Reduces the mid-range frequencies, often used in metal for a heavy sound.

Arrangement & Mixing Techniques

These keywords relate to how different parts are placed and interact within the song.

Keyword	Description
Autotune	Applies the modern, robotic, and perfectly-in-tune vocal effect.
Double-Tracking	Layering the same performance (especially vocals or guitar) to create a fuller, richer sound.
Sidechaining	Creates a "pumping" effect where the music "ducks" in volume when the kick drum hits. Essential for EDM.
Stereo Imaging	Describes how sounds are placed in the left and right speakers. Use "Wide Stereo" for a big, spacious feel.

Appendix I: Arrangement & Performance

Use these keywords in your Style Prompts to guide *how* the instruments are played and how the song is structured. These terms help you act as the band's director, shaping the overall performance.

Rhythmic Foundation & Groove

These keywords describe the feel and style of the rhythm section.

Keyword	Description
Beat Drop	The moment in a dance track where the rhythm kicks in with full force.
Driving Beat	A rhythm with strong, forward momentum that pushes the song along.
Four-on-the-Floor	The classic dance beat where the kick drum hits on every beat (1-2-3-4).
Groove	The overall rhythmic "feel" of the song that makes you want to move.
Offbeat Rhythm	A rhythm that emphasizes the beats *between* the main pulses, common in reggae.
Steady Beat	A consistent, simple, and reliable rhythm; not too complex.
Syncopated Rhythm	A funky rhythm with accents on unexpected beats.

Melodic & Harmonic Elements

These keywords define the character of the song's main musical ideas.

Keyword	Description

Arpeggio	Playing the notes of a chord one by one in a rising or falling pattern.
Call and Response	An arrangement where one musical phrase (the "call") is answered by another.
Catchy Hook	The most memorable musical or lyrical phrase of the song; the part you can't forget.
Catchy Melody	A tune that is memorable and easy to sing or hum along to.
Counter-Melody	A secondary melody played at the same time as the main melody.
Power Chords	Simple, heavy-sounding guitar chords essential for rock and metal.
Riff	A short, repeated, and memorable musical phrase, often played by a guitar or piano.
Soaring Melody	A melody that rises dramatically in pitch, creating an epic or emotional feeling.
Vocal Harmonies	Background vocals that sing different notes to support and enrich the lead vocal.

Performance Dynamics & Energy Flow

Use these keywords to control the song's energy level from start to finish.

Keyword	Description
Acoustic Arrangement	Specifies a version of a song played on non-electric instruments like acoustic guitar.
Anthemic	A big, powerful, and epic sound designed for a large crowd to sing along to.
Build / Build-up	A section where the intensity, volume, and number of instruments gradually increase.
Dynamic Contrast	A performance that features significant and noticeable changes between loud and soft sections.
Live Feel	Sounds like a live concert recording rather than a perfectly polished studio track.
Orchestral Arrangement	A version of a song arranged for a full orchestra with strings, horns, etc.

Overall Performance Style

These keywords describe how the virtual "band" plays together.

Keyword	Description
Improvised	Gives the music a spontaneous, unplanned feel, as if the musicians are making it up on the spot.
Intricate	A complex performance with many detailed and interwoven parts.
Laid-back	A relaxed, behind-the-beat rhythmic feel; not rushed.
Loose	A relaxed performance style where the timing is not perfectly rigid.
Playful	A lighthearted and fun performance style.
Tight	A precise and perfectly-in-sync performance where all musicians sound locked together.

www.ingramcontent.com/pod-product-compliance
Lightning Source LLC
Chambersburg PA
CBHW050310230526
45471CB00005B/2106